In the Slipstream of Time

by

Tom Kiske

"In the Slipstream of Time," by Tom Kiske. ISBN 978-1-63868-153-3 (softcover).

Published 2023 by Virtualbookworm.com Publishing Inc., P.O. Box 9949, College Station, TX 77842, US. ©2023, Tom Kiske.

Books by Tom Kiske

Time has its own Terms

Tales in Ordinary Time

Welcome to Happy-Land

Prostate Cancer: A Fighting Man's Guide (E-book)

Dedication

As The Shirelles sang back in 1961:

"This is dedicated to the one I love."

("Each night before you go to bed, my baby
Whisper a little prayer for me, my baby
And tell all the stars above:
This is dedicated to the one I love.")

Table of Contents

𝓟reface

HEREIN YOU WILL FIND A WODGE, bunch or heap of essays, snippets, sketches, random thoughts and even some short poems. Mostly, they're essays, making me (at least in my mind) an essayist. E.B. White says "The essayist is a self-liberated man, sustained by the childish belief that everything he thinks about, everything that happens to him, is of general interest." He adds, "Only a person who is congenitally self-centered has the effrontery and the stamina to write essays."

While I can't disagree with the estimable E.B., others have described essayists in terms less damaging to the ego. R.B. O'Brien says, "*I write to re-write the moments I've lived in a way that makes more sense to me.*" Someone (I've been unable to find the exact quote) said he felt the need to 'get it all down' or he'd be held personally responsible. I feel the same – as though it's my duty to commit certain things to writing, especially things relating to the times in which I've lived. I cannot explain why, but I feel a deep concern that the way things were during my lifetime not be forgotten; that not only major events – the domain of historians – are important, but also what life was like for a common, undistinguished American, from the 1940's to 2023. What he experienced, what he thought about, what he felt.

I hope I've done so in a manner that holds your interest, is somewhat entertaining, and maybe makes you pause for a moment to think about something you might otherwise have never considered. Some of these brief tales, I hope, will bring a chuckle.

Lastly, this: some of these essays are so short as to hardly qualify for inclusion in that genre. Maybe they're just fragments. But they're moments that arrested me. Made me stop whatever I was doing, pause and reflect on what underlying import they might have. Or maybe it was apophenia, assigning a meaning to some random occurrence, inferring a pattern where none existed. Like seeing Jesus's face on a piece of toast.

Regardless, I hope you won't just skim the words and flip the page. I hope you'll find something here that will make you stop reading, close the book and maybe conjure up your own interpretation of what I've attempted to capture. Either that or cause you to recall a golden moment you experienced. Or make you a bit more alert to the possibility of such moments in your life.

The Legend of the Yellow-Jacketed Stranger

Who was that yellow-jacketed Stranger?
Anonymous wedding guest

It was not long after graduation and thus the heart of the Wedding Season. It seemed almost every week brought an invitation to some friend's nuptials, many of which were from "friends" I barely recalled. These were easily dispatched by sending a congratulatory card plus the perfunctory gift or else simply ignored. One invitation, however, stood out from the rest. My college roommate and one of my best friends was marrying his high school sweetheart and I was to be a groomsman.

Attending a wedding was not among my favorite things to do and being part of one, no matter how minor my role, filled me with apprehension. Still, this was Alex. I was looking forward to seeing him again and curious about the girl he'd chosen, so this was a Don't Miss event.

I was already married by then and our firstborn was still an infant, which meant I'd be making the drive from St. Louis to Kansas City alone as Paula remained at home to care for our daughter. As was often the case back then, on the day I was to head out, I was running late. I'd rented a white jacket tuxedo sight unseen from a little storefront place that had but one thing to recommend it: it was close to where we lived, actually right on my way out of town. I ran in quickly, paid, grabbed the black garment bag and hung it in the back seat of my '61 Chevy convertible before racing out of town.

As it turned out, I only made half the drive alone. Stopping mid-state in Columbia I ran across another mutual roommate who was at loose ends. I was certain Alex would be happy to see Steve again and I was glad to have company for the rest of the trip, so off we went on I70 west, me and my wedding date - or in today's parlance, my "Plus One."

My recollection is a little cloudy on exactly how we spent most of the day before the wedding once we hooked up with Alex and our other buddy - and my fellow groomsman - Bob. This was long before bachelor parties became a thing, so it's likely we just grabbed a bite, then played a few games of pool or something, but I can't be sure. I remember vividly how the evening ended, tho. We'd driven Alex home and were sitting in the car outside his house reluctant to part company. One of us asked Alex if he might perhaps be able to lay his hands on some adult beverages. He ran up to check, then returned with a few six packs of beer that had been sitting out on his porch. Unrefrigerated beer. Warm beer. Fine with us. We sat there in the car talking, reminiscing, laughing and polishing off Alex's beer.

We spent the night at the home of Alex's parents and morning, as you'll imagine, came way too soon. It was to be an early wedding and we were all still pretty woozy when it came time to don our tuxes. Alex, along with Bob and the rest of the groomsmen had these brilliant, dazzlingly incandescent white jackets that looked as if they'd never been worn before and might scorch the retina of anyone who gazed directly at them too long without protective eye wear.

Then there was mine. When I pulled it out of the garment bag it didn't quite meet the white jacket standard. In fact, it looked like something from Antiques Roadshow. Every seam was worn and yellowed with age. The whole thing was only white in the sense that it wasn't black or brown and once upon a time, perhaps in a previous century, might have been white. Now it better approximated the hue of a weathered antebellum manuscript or a disintegrating parchment scroll recovered from the Great Pyramid.

Nevertheless, this was the tuxedo I had and thus the tuxedo I put on despite my buddies' quizzical expressions and barely-stifled snickers and chuckles. So, at the appointed time, Alex and his groomsmen took their assigned places, standing at the front of the packed church, most of us still a bit warm-beer wobbly and not exactly fresh-faced with youthful glow. In fact, the muted hue of my off-color jacket at least provided a somewhat less stark contrast than those brilliant white ones to our sallow, sickly faces. It offered me small comfort.

Regardless, despite our hangovers and my profound chromatic embarrassment, we somehow made it through the ceremony. None of us fell over, regurgitated or otherwise publicly humiliated the newlyweds beyond some too-audible gastrointestinal rumblings. We got our buddy married to the lovely Martha. After the reception the bride and groom departed to privately celebrate a union that remains intact to this day, 54 years later. Steve, Bob and I took advantage of Alex's parents' generous offer to spend another night at their home. The next morning, too soon we all headed our separate ways. It was a few weeks later that Alex reached out, thanking us for our participation and reporting bemusedly that several of the people who'd attended the wedding had approached him to ask, "Who was that yellow-jacketed stranger?"

This is how it was that a legend was born and how for many years, at least among a select group of friends and wedding guests, I became known as – well, you know.

Our Space

Our space is small

Our time is brief

We grow what beauty we can

Planting roots deep in the soil

And dreams high in the clouds

We labor, sing, sleep

And love,

       Seeking what is right and true

Within our vision's range

No matter what the limits be

We do, we are

We live

This now

This always living now.

It's the Eyes

"Jeepers creepers, where'd ya get those peepers?"
Mercer & Warren

Thinking this morning of a girl whose name I cannot recall. She sat next to me in a class at Mizzou. It was one of those huge lecture halls - hundreds of kids in theater-style seating, trying with varying degrees of success to pay attention and take notes as some tenured professor who'd long ago lost interest in his subject droned on. It was an environment where it was easy to let your attention drift, and as we were all young the direction of drift can easily be surmised.

I do not remember how many days we sat side by side before the young lady ventured to speak to me. I expect it was early in the semester, likely the first or second week of classes. I do know that it was she, not I, who initiated what became an ongoing conversation, albeit one conducted in the hushed and secretive tones necessary to avoid detection by the stage-strutting martinet to whom we were supposed to be listening.

I thought little of the developing relationship and in fact did not see it as such. It was just mildly pleasant to have someone nearby with whom to exchange brief comments, usually critiquing the professor or the subject matter. I came and went from the lecture hall with little thought outside it of the girl.

I came to understand that for her it was different.

There came a day in which she arrived at her designated place visibly upset. I asked her what was the matter and she blurted out something about a friend having been killed in Vietnam. Then she fled the room sobbing.

It seemed the right thing to do was follow her out and, in all innocence, or perhaps naivete I did so, thinking only to provide a measure of understanding and sympathy.

And so, on a little tree-lined plaza just outside, we sat and talked. She provided few details about her friend, the circumstances of his death or what memorial services might demand her presence. She wanted to talk about other things, presumably, I thought, to take her mind off her grief.

In the course of our conversation, she discovered that I lived in an apartment off campus. She proposed that we "take a little ride out there."

Maybe you can guess where this is going, but don't get ahead of the story.

Thinking back, I ask myself whether, as we sat there on that plaza, I might've perhaps put my arm around her in consolation or offered some sign of affection beyond the scope of someone wishing to be of help to an acquaintance. My recollection is insufficiently clear to justify a claim of absolute innocence in this regard, but I know it was not my intent to suggest the possibility of romance.

Still, we did end up in the apartment I shared with three buddies, none of whom was then present. It was a nice apartment, new and somewhat upscale by the modest standards of 1960's Columbia, Missouri. The girl was impressed.

She took my hand and gazed into my eyes. "You know," she said, "I could stay here. I could cook for you."

Finally, the light dawned on me. Finally, I knew what this girl was looking for. Had there been signs before, signs to which I'd been stupidly oblivious?

I don't know. Probably. But now the cards were on the table. My bedroom was only a few steps from where we stood. A few easy steps, it would seem.

But they were steps not taken.

I can't remember what words I employed to deflect what was looming and instead usher the girl from my apartment. I'm certain I was gentle with her. I'm equally certain she was nonetheless disappointed and hurt.

We drove to her dorm without much talk. Before she left the car she said, "It's the eyes, isn't it?"

She was not an unattractive girl, but her eyes were not her best feature. A little too small, perhaps, for her face. I don't know. Something.

I told her she was wrong, assured her that was not it at all, but I know she didn't believe me.

She got out of the car, walked slowly away and disappeared into her dorm. Although I'd done nothing wrong, I felt a heavy guilt and a pervasive, lingering sadness.

All these years later I feel it still - whenever I think of the girl whose name I can't recall.

The Last Banana

The last banana
Sad and pining for the bunch
One shriveled old banana
It will not last 'til lunch
-
Once yellow, this banana
Now marked with brown age spots
But still a good banana
Only banana that I gots
-
I love you, last banana
Don't see your kind as others see 'em
More than just another fruit
But a fine source of potassium
-
Now a fitting end for you, banana
A moment quite ethereal
Peeled, sliced and in a bowl
A lovely topping for my cereal

Oh, little last banana
Gone without a trace
I wish that I'd done more
At least, you know, said Grace.

February, Blah.

February is meteorologically miserable where I live. We usually don't get buckets of rain, it's just cloudy, gray, foggy, misty and, well, miserable. Sorta like San Francisco except, you know, without the ocean, the bridge and the cable cars.

The sun peeked out here exactly once early in the month and then like a celestial Punxatawney Phil, ducked back behind the clouds for the next few weeks. If you took a poll right now February would get a very low approval rating. Possibly even lower than Congress.

Maybe it's time to consider calendar reform, starting with February. We've been stuck with the Gregorian Calendar since 1582 and frankly, it's showing its age. For one thing, it's not precise enough for the modern era - off from the true solar year by 26 seconds. That might've been a trivial error 436 years ago but it's huge in the internet age. How many tweets can a tweeter tweet in 26 seconds? Your average pre-teen - or notorious ex-President - could probably crank out half a dozen or so.

We can't fix the whole calendar at once, but February seems most in need of some serious upgrading. For one thing, with only 28 days it's the runt of the litter, so to speak. Black History Month deserves better. Maybe it's time to move that to March and demote February to dwarf status like scientists did with Pluto a while ago.

Then, too, February's spelled funny. It's got that extra "r" that just seems wrong. We say "Feb you airy," right? Not "Feb brew airy." Admittedly, that superfluous "r" seems vaguely Texan. Like we say "Perd nallis" for Pedernales. Really though, it's Latin. From "Februarius mensis" or "month of purification."

But what the heck are we purifying these days? If we could use February to sanitize our political mess, I suppose we could justify sticking with the name. Otherwise, maybe we ought to go back to the Old English "solomonad" or "mud month." That seems more like it. "Blah month" would be better, but that wasn't in the Old English lexicon. Mud or Blah, it's still winter. It's a cold, gloomy month you just want to get through as best you can. If things weren't dreary enough, football season's over. That leaves February with one bright spot: Valentine's.

Sadly, that poor guy is barely hanging on to sainthood. Turns out there were three dudes named Valentine and nobody's quite sure which one the holiday commemorates. Church authorities quietly pulled Valentine from The General Roman Calendar in 1969 and seem a little embarrassed by some of the off-color shenanigans his day inspires. They'd probably kick him out of the club entirely except it would outrage and possibly bankrupt the folks who sell greeting cards, flowers, candy and skimpy lingerie.

What else is in February? Well, there's Presidents Day, but that holiday lost a lot of luster when Congress whittled it down from Washington's birthday and Lincoln's. Presidents Day strikes many as bland and generic. Kind of blah. Some of our Presidents have been blah, too. A few were worse than blah. Why celebrate those guys?

Then there's Groundhog Day. Folks in Pennsylvania might be miffed over losing that one, but even they know it's not a real holiday because you don't get off work. Besides, when you think about it that shadow-seeing ritual is statistically dismal. Half the time Punxatawney Phil is going to predict winter dragging on six more weeks. How depressing. Do we need that?

No, we'd clearly be better off without February. Put those 28 days to better use. Add a couple of bonus holidays after January 1 to ease the grim return to work. Sprinkle the rest through the year as designated play days. As a bonus, by dropping February we'd simplify that "30 days hath September, April, June and November" thing. No more awkward "except February, which has 28." That always seemed like an afterthought anyway. Plus, it's not even right. The real program's way more complex. You have that extra day wedged in every 4 years - except years divisible by 100 - unless they're also divisible by 400. Leap Year. Who dreamed up a calendar you need algebra to figure out? Reason enough to drop February.

But what if you were born in the Dwarf Month? Simple. Just pick a different birthday. Any one you want. Want to be younger, switch your birthday to later in the year. Want to qualify sooner for your driver's license, move your birthday up to January. Everybody's happy.

So, the only real hang-up to dumping February is the popularity and commercial impact of Valentines Day. Fortunately, there's an elegant solution sure to sweeten things up for merchants and romantics. Merge Valentine's with St. Patrick's Day. Now that would be a day to really celebrate!

Finally, let's take a hard look at the rest of the months, starting with their names. They're old and boring. Nobody knows what they mean anymore or where they came from. They're long and hard to spell. They're not in alphabetical order nor are they decimal-friendly. Here's what we do: cut back to ten months. Name them after Snow White and the seven dwarves. Plus one to grow on and, of course, Truck Month.

The Blücher[1] English Dictionary

FOR IMMEDIATE RELEASE - April 1, 2022

The Blücher English Dictionary is pleased to announce the opening of The E. Fudd Home for Worn-out Words (HWOW!)

Although that other shoe style dictionary each year proclaims a new "word of the year" added to the lexicon, at Blücher we believe it equally important to recognize certain words that have earned retirement. Retired status may be achieved through overuse, misuse, confusion or just plain public weariness. The E. Fudd Home for Worn-out Words now provides a pleasant environment for retired words (and phrases!) to live out the remainder of their pitiful lives without bugging the heck out of the English-speaking human population.

Accordingly, the primary or platinum level Inductee for 2021 is:

fraught

Fraught earned retirement through both overuse and misuse. Fraught is an adjective meaning "loaded." Proper usage demands the term be followed with the preposition "with" and a noun designating what something was loaded with, often "peril." Absent the noun, we're left to wonder, loaded with *what*? Happiness? Joy? Potatoes?

---

[1]*NOTE: Like Oxford, Blücher is a dictionary and a shoe style. It is also a word which, spoken aloud with the German pronunciation, strikes terror into members of Genus Equus.*

See, nothing can be just fraught. It really should be fraught with something. Failing that, the term devolves into mere blather. Possibly this accounts for the astonishing popularity the word enjoyed during 2021, a year fraught with fraught.

Over-fraught, to be completely honest.

Although there were many geriatric candidates well qualified for retirement, as First Runner-up - which will serve in the event the Primary is unable to do so - we have chosen:

F-k
(the "F-word")

The F-word rarely appears in serious print publications, it is ubiquitous in most movie categories and, most often as "F--king", in performances by stand-up comics. In movies, the term is used for shock value and to add emphasis. However, in 2021 it was used so often that it no longer shocks, nor does it add emphasis. It's reduced to the status of a verbal tic, like "uh" or among younger generations, "like."

Comics, on the other hand, employ "F-king" in hopes it will somehow render an otherwise humorless statement funny. For example, instead of "Have you ever lost one of your socks," a comic might ask, "Have you ever lost one of your f-king socks?" Way funnier, at least in the mind of a stand-up comic. But if the term ever possessed comedic powers, they're certainly lost when "f-king" peppers every other sentence. Time for it to take a serious f-king tour of the E. Fudd Home for Worn-out Words.

Dishonorable Mention awards were presented to the following weary words:

optics
at the end of the day
take it to the next level
epicenter
pivot
quantum leap
begs the question
failure is not an option

proactive

The E. Fudd Home has reserved a separate but equal wing for phrases, which earn retirement based on how annoying they are. For 2021, even though the phrase is restricted to telephone answering machines or services, the unanimous choice for most annoying phrase was:

"We're experiencing unusual call volume"

The Retirement Committee hasn't provided further detail regarding their choice as they felt it speaks for itself.

Although voting has concluded for 2021, nominations for words and phrases to be retired for 2022 may be submitted to the E. Fudd Home for Worn-out Words - monetary donations gladly accepted.

Happiness

I think that if you ever pause
in whatever you're doing
        And ask yourself
if you're happy
        You probably are

        But if you didn't ask
Maybe you wouldn't know.

Alleys Are My Beat

As a kid in the old South St. Louis neighborhood, back alleys were my beat. My domain ran two blocks, from behind my house at 11ᵗʰ & Victor north to Lami. Although my pals and I enjoyed playing cork ball and bottles, I was partial to more free-wheeling activities.

I learned to ride a two-wheeler in my alley. The brand-new Schwin I'd gotten one Christmas sat neglected in our basement until Spring Cleaning when my parents dragged it out and leaned it up against a pole in the back yard. Whatever training exercise my dad may have attempted earlier had proven unsuccessful. Instead, I learned by accident. I climbed aboard, held on to the pole and eased my bike back and forth. Harmless fun until I pushed a little too far forward and had to let go of the pole.

I was *riding* but now what? At the end of the yard, I managed to execute a 180, headed out to Victor, down to my alley, then north. When I reached Barton there was no traffic so I zipped right across to the next block. Everything was going great until I approached Lami. Picturing the steep hill beyond, which led to busy Shenandoah I realized I had no idea how to stop this contraption. Like most kids, though, I was skilled at crude but effective innovation, rescuing myself from certain death by engineering a semi-controlled crash into the side of a garage. Not awful for a first-time cyclist.

Then there was the time my friends and I discovered a large snapping turtle on the vacant lot across from my house. For reasons known only to small boys my buddy Bryan felt the turtle would be much happier at his house. Among other things it would confer upon him as Turtlemaster a greatly enhanced stature in kiddom. The reluctant reptile was induced to go along with the plan in this way: Bryan would wave a broomstick handle in the turtle's face until the powerful jaws snapped on it, allowing Bryan to drag it two feet or so down the alley. It must've taken half an hour or more to navigate the two blocks to Bryan's house while a growing entourage of fascinated kids followed the slow parade. It was to prove an unhappy journey for the snapper. A few days later I asked Bryan how his turtle was doing. "Aw," he said, "My old man-made soup out of it."

It was a few years later when an alley was the scene of a scary but seductive pre-adolescent nighttime invitation to adventure. A friend and I had gone to the New Shenandoah (later the Apache) theater on Broadway to see the latest thriller, <u>The Creeper</u>, a truly lame movie about a shadowy, threatening character who lurked in - of course - alleys. It was likely around 10 pm when, having left my friend at his house, I was walking home alone, a bit anxious about possible South St. Louis Creepers. As I passed the alley around Tenth and Lami a girl's voice called alluringly from the alley. "Hey," she asked, "Wanna kiss?"

Then there was some muted giggling and another girl called out, "Yeah, handsome, you wanna smooch?"

I admit I paused a second or two before silently walking on, fearful of some kind of Creeper trick. It was an adventure that was not to be. Had I seen a different movie, though, who knows?

Deepak Chopra vs the Zombies

So, I got this book from the library: <u>Resurrecting the Soul</u>, by Deepak Chopra. Thought I might find something worthwhile in the book despite prior disappointment with the author's work. 'Twas not to be. Opening the book, one of the early chapters is entitled "The Body is a Fiction." Instant bullshit alert. If my body is a fiction, Mr. Chopra, then of course my eyes are part of that fiction. Fictional eyes can't read your book, can they?

I just hope this doesn't mean my soul won't be resurrected. Frankly, though, I'm not sure it's in need of resurrecting at the moment. I'm not dead and don't think my soul is, either. Too often ignored, perhaps, possibly to the point of being thought moribund. But dead? No, no, no.

Good thing, too. Christmas season would be an awful time to be dragging around a dead soul. Why, you'd be little more than a zombie, and as we know, Christmas Ain't for Zombies. Boy, that would make a good bumper sticker, huh?

Still, if you were called upon to prove you weren't a soul-less zombie, could you do so? Let's say you were in the military and that "Don't Ask, Don't Tell" thing was extended to include zombie-ism. If you were summoned before a tribunal, what evidence could you produce to refute the allegation of zombiehood? Well, as my wife might say, let's make a little list -

Proof I Am Not a Zombie

1. Walking. I walk fairly normally. Maybe not with that cool, Travolta Saturday Night Fever swagger of old, but still a cut above the halting, stumbling shuffle you see with zombies. You can always tell a zombie by the lurch.

2. I eat and drink regular food and beverages. Zombies are known to subsist on a rather restrictive diet of human flesh, with maybe a brain thrown in on special occasions. They're pretty much exempt from the obesity epidemic.

3. I enjoy music, including rock and roll. You've never seen a dancing zombie, have you?* OK, technically I haven't done a lot of dancing lately myself, but I do bounce around in my car seat when something good comes on the radio. "Poke Salad Annie," for example.

4. I do not bear the stench of the open grave. At least not on bath day.

5. My clothes are not in tatters. Really, they're not. A little old, perhaps, not the latest fashion, but certainly not the ragged-and-encrusted-with-graveyard-soil grunge look zombies seem to prefer.

6. I still like girls. Zombies don't seem to have much of a sex life. Not known as big flirts, for example. This is not to imply zombies are gay. Boy, "gay zombie" calls to mind a really weird image, doesn't it?

7. I am gainfully employed. What kind of job is a zombie qualified for? You never even see them as Wal-Mart greeters. I guess a zombie could get hired as a telemarketer, but he'd have to work on diction. "Arrrrrr" just wouldn't cut it.

8. I drive a car. I don't think zombies can even get a drivers license. Wonder what they use for a photo ID?

9. I'm not afraid of garlic, holy water or crucifixes, nor do I spontaneously combust when exposed to sunlight. Wait, maybe I've

confused zombies with vampires. Vampires are the ones in those "Twilight" movies, right? Zombies are the ones who *watch* those movies.

10. I laugh. A lot. Zombies are a humorless lot. Heck, I bet a zombie could probably read this whole list and not crack a grin. A priest, a rabbi and a zombie go into this bar . . ..

I think this should suffice for an acquittal. To paraphrase Tricky Dick, I am NOT a zombie!

----

*NOTE: There was that "Thriller" video on MTV, but I'm pretty sure those were actors.

A morning conversation
With the girl in the dry cleaners:
It's cold
Very cold
Yesterday was colder
I worry for my peppers
It's speech with no significance
Never to be recalled
It's just what people do
Because silence is cold
Very cold
But yesterday was colder.

Work

"Hard work never killed anyone, but why take a chance?"
Edgar Bergen

Not to take anything away from the youth of today, but kids in the 1950's and 60's *worked*. We were broken in, so to speak, by household chores. Mine were:

- Set the table for dinner
- Dry the dishes afterward (my Dad usually washed)
- Take the trash can out to the curb on trash day, then bring it back after it was emptied into the big truck.

No big deal – unless you forgot one! Assuming you were diligent though, your duties earned you a weekly allowance; a quarter, maybe, or even a half-dollar. You could buy comic books!

There was work at school, too. The job of Patrol Boy was actually a prestigious one you might be chosen for in 7th grade. You wore (rolled up on your hip, to be cool) a white, garrison-type canvas belt and bandolier, on which you pinned your badge. Yes, you got to wear an actual chrome metal badge just like the cops!

As a Patrol Boy (no girls), you had a serious responsibility: it was your duty to make sure the little kids made it safely across the street intersections near school. At my school, at least, we took this job seriously. We were rewarded for our service by being allowed to leave class early to get to our assigned posts, and when the bell rang in the morning, we could be a little late for class. Also, once a year we got to attend a Cardinals baseball game for free, courtesy of AAA, which sponsored the safety patrol program nationwide.

Later, in high school, the cafeteria offered an entre for some of us to acquire an earning experience as well as a learning one. My friend Warren washed dishes for 6 "chips" a day, while Mitch and I were paid the same for coming in early in the morning to stack stools atop the tables so the floor could be mopped. In typical kid fashion, we make a game of it: Mitch took half the cafeteria and I took the other half and we'd race to see who could get the job done first. Six chips was exactly enough to buy lunch.

My buddies and I took another job that paid in fun and perks rather than chips or cash; we volunteered to be "registration clerks." Back in our day, registration day took place just before a new semester began. Kids had to go to a certain desk in a certain room sign up for each class they wanted to take. My buddies and I manned those desks. Why? Because we got first choice for the specific classes we wanted, and we could put whomever we wanted in *our* class. This meant we and all our friends ended up in the same class, often to the dismay of our teachers, *and* that our class had all the cute girls.

When it came to work outside of school, things got more complicated. You had to get a work permit. This involved showing up in person at the Board of Education, filling out forms and answering a bunch of questions, like "Do you have syphilis?"

Once you passed that hurdle though, it got easier. I attended an inner-city high school, McKinley, where the administration recognized that many of their students needed to work, either for reasons of their own or because they were expected to contribute to their family situation. As a result, the school had developed a few connections with businesses in the community. Moreover, McKinley had a program called Distributed Education (DE for short) whereby kids could be dismissed early, say 2:00 to work at an approved company.

Outside of that, a number of companies made it a point to hire McKinleyites. Fouke and Fox come to mind. Fouke Fur Company provided temporary work for a dozen or so boys once a year when the buyers came to town. These were great jobs for at least three reasons:

1. We got off school for a few days to work there,
2. It was a link to St. Louis's fur trading history, and
3. The buyers tipped really well.

There was a fourth reason, too – the work wasn't that hard. Basically, you just flipped pelts out one at a time from a big stack, then folded 'em back up and put 'em away after the buyer examined each one. We liked to joke that it was a "hairy" job, but some kids went on to work full time at Fouke.

The big Fox Theater offered McKinley girls work at the candy counter in the main lobby. I can't be sure if appearance was a hiring criterion, but it sure seemed all the candy girls were good-looking. I know I spend more money (and time) at the Fox candy counter than any other movie theater.

Spiro found the sweetest gig ever just down Grand Avenue from the Fox at the old St. Louis Theater (now Powell Hall). After working there a few days one summer as an usher, the assistant manager made him an offer he couldn't refuse: don't bother showing up for work. I'll fill out your time cards and we'll split your paycheck 50-50.

This deal worked out well until the manager caught on and demanded all the ushers show up in uniform late one afternoon. Spiro was at football practice and couldn't make it, so he was fired from the easiest job he ever had.

Schneider Packing Company, down below Broadway, was another place that favored McKinley kids. Johnny M. worked in the office there in the early 50's, and Warren took over that job later in the same decade, typing letters, collecting "kill sheets" and calculating price-per-pound yields. Warren also found summer work at a gas station in the Missouri bootheel and supplemented his earnings with several odd jobs, including shingling a roof, painting rooms, umpiring Little League games and, as he phrased it, "polluting the dirt roads around town with used motor oil to keep the dust down."

Several kids worked at neighborhood grocery stores or butcher shops. Johnny M. was a stock boy and cashier at Boyers at Menard and Barton; Joe P worked at a butcher shop near Soulard Market and Bryan delivered groceries for Wagner's. Kids whose parents owned stores often found themselves conscripted into unpaid (or low-paid) servitude. Gloria and Angelica were among their unfortunate number at their dad's place on 7th Street, and Bill S.

claims he was "...enslaved in my parents' store from the age of five until my release in my late teen years."

One of our teachers recommended my friend, Mitch, and me to a relative who was part-owner of Sunshine Laundry. Our summer job was to lug carpets from one storage location to a new one. Many of these rugs had been stored for more than a few years and were, well, filthy. Hauling them around was dirty, hot and hard work for sixty-five cents an hour. It was a truly lousy job, but it came with two benefits. All that lifting built a well-developed set of biceps. More importantly, though, because we ate lunch at Mitch's house, I got to meet his lovely younger sister, Laura.

I also worked after school and Saturdays at Soulard Branch Library, which was a lot cleaner than the laundry and offered at least a modicum of intellectual challenge as well. There were two other nice features about the job. First, the McKinley GAA (Girl's Athletic Association) sometimes met in the basement of the building and I became skilled at manufacturing excuses to wander downstairs. Secondly, one of the librarians hired her neighbor's attractive teenage daughter, Karen, to work one summer. Need I say more?

Kids I knew found all kinds of jobs. Some worked at local dime stores, clothing stores, drug stores and in bowling alleys as pin spotters until that gig was abolished by machines. Steak 'n Shake offered the opportunity to work as a car hop for a buck a night plus tips. Those tips could add up to as much as $50 a week or so, which was not bad money back then.

Wherever you worked, if at all possible, you were obligated to cut another McKinley kid a break. I recall going with Warren to the Highlands swimming pool. A girl we knew from school was working the ticket counter, where a turnstile-controlled entry. She took a quick glance around to make sure nobody was looking, then whispered "Jump over!" We got in free!

Today, many parents are sufficiently affluent that their children don't have to work as we did back in the dark ages. I suppose that's okay; maybe it's a sign of progress. But I wonder if these kids aren't missing out on something. There are lessons a job teaches that can be found in no classroom or book: punctuality, industry and perhaps most importantly, the value of a dollar. Once you realize how long and hard you have to work to earn a buck, you're far less likely to squander it on foolishness. Well, unless you're a congressman or hedge fund manager.

From my experience and from others I've spoken with, it seems most of us look back on our school jobs with a degree of nostalgic pride. It could be, of course, simply because we survived them and because they're behind us now. But more than that, I think it's because the jobs we held long ago became part of who we are.

And they remain part of us still.

Sinister Slithering

Something there is instinctively terrifying about a snake. Not a captive, zoo snake securely sealed behind a thick glass barrier, but an outdoor, wild snake in reasonable proximity to your ill-protected and vulnerable calf. The snake's very means of locomotion seems unnatural, sinister. A snake does not walk, run, hop, skip, swim or (thank goodness) fly. Snakes slither. They coil. They move with that unique and disturbing undulating motion that doesn't seem sufficient to propel them, yet they do manage to go from here to there - or worse, from there to here - without difficulty. And they do so expeditiously. Snakes are *fast*. And from that warning coiled position, they *strike!*

Only a small number of snakes, we're told, are poisonous, but they all *look* dangerous. It's hard for the lay, non-herpetologically-inclined person to distinguish a venomous snake from one whose fangs are less likely to prove lethal. You'd have to approach perilously close to the subject serpent and who wants to chance that?

Snakes serve their purpose in nature's grand scheme, I'm sure. They consume other pests. Probably their repertoire includes other less known but equally beneficial activities as well. Surely though, such functions might've been assigned less evil-looking creatures. Ones that slither not nor do they coil. Perhaps a mammal could do the job. One of our own, so to speak. A familiar member of our own taxonomic class, Mammalia. Preferably a gentle, fur-bearing mammal content with domestication. The puppy comes to mind.

Put me down as favoring more puppies and fewer snakes. An outright snake ban would not offend my environmental sensibilities in the least. It is said that nature abhors a vacuum. Well, *my* nature abhors a snake.

Then there's this: snakes have some sort of zombie-like life force. It's hard to kill a snake. With most animals, decapitation does the trick. With snakes, though, you sever the head, you end up with two problems. Two seemingly live - or at least undead - problems. The body keeps wriggling around and the head - get this! - the head keeps snapping, trying to bite you! Needless to say, this is very unsettling. If movies are to be believed, a dead person takes a while to re-animate and become a zombie. You get a little breathing room. Not so for snakes. Kill 'em, they come back immediately! I don't know why the rules are different for snake zombies but it seems really unfair.

It is for these reasons that rather than deal myself with the water moccasin in my back yard, I summoned the professionals from College Station Animal Control. Admittedly, less damage might've been inflicted on my he-man self-image had the pro snake wrestlers not turned out to be two young girls, and had the water moccasin not turned out to be a "harmless" yellow-bellied water snake, but really, it wasn't that I was scared. No, I was just operating from a mature and totally reasonable abundance of caution. Prudence. Discretion.

No, really.

A Thousand Words a Minute

I didn't do it and I'll never do it again.
Universal Excuse

One of the many things in which I take zero pride is the fact I can read a thousand words a minute. I'm not bragging. I'm not making it up, either. Its documented, it's even been the subject of a newspaper article. Really, tho, it's kinda dumb and I'd rather forget about it. Nevertheless, it's a story, so . . .

In the Fall of 1961, Bob and I entered Washington University. The school is not in DC. It's not in Washington State. It's in St. Louis and back then Wash U. liked to refer to itself as The Harvard of the Midwest. Pretentious? You bet, but a good school with a student body comprised in large part of kids not quite bright enough, connected enough or adept enough at self-promotion to qualify as material for the real Harvard. Kids from all over; not many from St. Louis. Bob and I, presumably "disadvantaged" graduates of a little inner-city high school, might've been part of some diversity program. Helped that we were both National Merit Scholars.

Anyway, as part of freshman orientation, we all had to take a reading test. The ubiquitous standardized test of that era: read a passage, then answer a bunch of multiple-choice questions about it. Turn the page & continue. When you're done, hand it in. Out of maybe a hundred kids in our session, Bob and I were the first to finish.

A few days later, we got quite a surprise. The campus newspaper ran a front-page article about the reading test. The headline read something like, "How fast can you Read? A Thousand Words a Minute is Possible!" In the article, I was stunned to find that it was Bob and me who were the champion speediest readers at (The Harvard of the Midwest). Nobody had called to provide the results of the reading test, nobody congratulated us; instead, we learned of our elevated status in the campus newspaper, which included our names.

Fortunately, the newspaper article was the extent of our brush with fame and immortality. There was no public ceremony; no prize, award or trophy was bestowed on us. We were both glad there wasn't more to-do about our reading prowess. This was not due to our innate humility. We knew the dark truth behind the story. Immortality? More like immorality. The newspaper article explained that the speed metric deducted points for wrong answers. Our look-back approach gave us a bit of a leg up on that part. Basically, we'd cheated.

In our defense, the cheating was unintentional, more the fault of poor testing protocol and instruction than any desire to deceive or vainglorious wish to distinguish ourselves by devious and dastardly deeds. See, to the best of my knowledge and recollection, neither the test booklet nor the proctor said anything about not looking back at the reading selection to answer the questions. So, we did.

Me first. Bob, sitting beside me, to his credit at least whispered to me, "Are you sure we can do that?" I hadn't seen or heard anything telling us not so, so I confidently assured him it was perfectly OK. Maybe it was my confidence or maybe the fact I'd scored a little higher than him on the SAT, but he shrugged and took my word for it.

I'd unwittingly enticed Bob into what could easily have escalated into a life of crime. Heck, he was already skilled at pitching pennies, an illicit but profitable endeavor he'd mastered in fierce lunchtime competition in the basement Boys Room at dear old McKinley High. If the Wash U career path didn't work out for him Bob might've become a bag man for the mob, or given his math skills, a Bernie Madoff style billionaire. Would that have been so bad? Assuming, that is, that he didn't get caught. It's that possibility that troubles me. If he had been apprehended, would my buddy have pointed the finger at me? Ratted me out in return for a reduced sentence? "It's all HIS fault," I imagine Bob pleading, "I was a GOOD boy until that damn Kiske led me astray!"

Who knows, instead of graduating college with bright futures and above-average earnings potential maybe we'd have ended up sharing a dank and dreary cell in the Jeff City Pen, condemned to while away the lonely years of our miserable confinement reading the Bible, the Bhagavad-Gita or old Bugs Bunny Comics.

At a thousand words a minute.

A Starry Night

It's a brief scene early in Cameron's <u>Titanic</u>: young Jack is resting on a bench on the ship's open deck. His eyes are on the sky and for a moment we see the vast expanse of stars as he does. The movie goes quickly on. I do not. I'm lost in thoughts of my father.

In 1943 or early '44, he's a US Marine shipping out to battle the Japanese in the south Pacific. He's aboard an aircraft carrier pressed into service as a troop transport. It's unbearably hot below deck where his bunk is and he's a bit claustrophobic as well, so he's found a spot topside, on the flight deck. At some point, like Jack, he must've let his mind wander among the endless array of stars, infinitely more than he'd ever seen. At 34, he'd never been far from his inner-city St. Louis neighborhood, where the sky is a narrow thing confined between buildings.

What thoughts coursed thru his mind as he lay there steaming in harm's way toward unknown dangers and an uncertain future? He's young, so there's the excitement of an adventure, but he's also left behind a wife and a newborn son he's only seen for a few days. His enlistment is for the duration of the war, so he doesn't know how long it will be until he sees his family again. He can't even be sure he'll survive to return to them. His worries are many.

Knowing my father, I'm certain his thoughts would've turned to God. His religious views were eclectic. He knew his Bible far more than most, but he was tolerant of other religious traditions and recognized the truths they offered as well. He knew the value of prayer. His son's birth was attended by his prayers, and now, thousands of miles from his family, he would've reached upward into that starry, starry night, asked that they be kept safe, asked that he be allowed to once again hold them in his arms.

My father survived World War II and lived a long life. Now he is many years gone, but he's never far away. Sometimes it's a simple thing that brings him close. Sometimes it's just a moment in a movie.

Something Awesome

Last week, when placing my lunch order at a local restaurant, the young lady behind the counter inquired, *"Is that for here or to go?"*

"Here," I replied.

"Awesome!" was her response.

She was evidently awed by my choice to dine in the establishment where she worked. Or perhaps it was my lack of hesitation reaching that crucial decision that left her awestruck. Either way, I found myself thinking, my goodness, this girl is very easily awed. She seemed a person of reasonable intelligence, and as many of our food emporia here in College Station employ A&M students, she may even have had a number of post-secondary credits bolstering her knowledge base. Yet she claimed to be awed by what seemed to me a mundane answer to a simple two-option multiple choice question.

Isn't awe usually the result of weightier matters? Wouldn't a better trained, more sensitive employee, noting my mature stature, have substituted, like, "groovy" or "far out?"

After all, my dictionary defines "awe" as "an emotion of mixed reverence, dread and wonder." It could also be "fearful veneration or respect." Certainly, I would expect the young lady to respect my decision to eat in rather than take out, but is it really the sort of thing that inspires reverence or wonder? And what could there possibly be in my simple *"here"* to make her fearful, fill her with dread? Is the food at this place really bad? Did she worry I'd become ill? Perhaps hurl?

But no, the girl's facial expression and tone of voice did not convey fear or dread. Rather, she was cheerful. Perky, one might say. The awe she felt must have been more on the reverence and wonder side of the definition.

Thinking back on the experience, tho, neither did the young lady seem greatly moved by this awesome event. She did not collapse in tears, nor raise her arms to heaven to mark the wondrous occasion. She didn't exclaim ecstatically to her co-workers, *"Oh, oh, the dude is eating IN!"* In fact, she seemed to display a great equanimity in the face of her self-confessed awe. Her life didn't seem much altered and altho I do not know this for fact, I suspect she did not resign her job and devote the remainder of her life to tasks more spiritual in nature than tapping lunch orders onto the keyboard of a point-of-sale computer. In fact, she just went right on to the next customer and took his order. I bet she repeated the query that launched my speculation, *"Is that for here or to go?"*

Maybe she found that customer's answer equally as awesome as mine. Or maybe it's only the *"here"* reply that invokes wonder. Maybe if the customer were to say *"To go,"* her mood would darken precipitously. Maybe instead of hearing a perky *"awesome"* the customer making the wrong choice would instead get a despondent *"Aw, crap!"*

I guess I could try it the next time I visit this restaurant, but I hate to put myself in the position of killing this young girl's buzz. There's enough sadness in the world, and if I can inspire awe with a simple *"here,"* isn't that one of those random acts of kindness we're encouraged to perform to make the world a better place?

What I worry about is that awe just ain't what it used to be. What was once an exceptionally powerful, potentially life-changing emotion seems now to be quite transitory and ephemeral. You get a little toke of awe, but then, whoosh, it's gone and you're aweless again, maybe craving your next hit. So, here's what I think: we all should practice giving awe every dang chance we get. Next time you visit a restaurant and somebody asks, *"For here or to go,"* be sure to say *"Here!"* Say it loud and say it proud. If we all did that, wouldn't it be, well, awesome?

𝒲𝒽𝒶𝓉 𝓡𝑒𝓂𝒶𝒾𝓃𝓈

Yesterday was a balmy 70-degree autumn day. This morning it is winter. 45 degrees and dropping. Gray skies and a blustery north wind. Change is upon us, change in its many aspects. In the weather and in the circumstances of our lives. Little around us remains constant. Even our bodies change, often not as we'd prefer.

What if anything remains the same? Is it, as the Gavin Rossdale song suggests, love? Sometimes, sometimes not, in my opinion. I believe love can grow or it can wither. Or following its own mystic nature, it may be lost for a time, then come 'round again to flower anew.

Such, though, is merely one form of love. The love between a man and a woman. Love that begins with romance but which may progress into something deeper and less prone to wandering or hiding or blowing away in the wind.

Even that more deeply-rooted love, though, may be merely a hue attaching to the real *thing* of love.

This is my hope and my belief: that love is *real*. Perhaps not tangible in the usual sense of the word, but nonetheless a thing we can perceive thru some undefined and seldom studied sense modality. It may be that it comes thru to us in different ways at different times of our lives. At twenty we are exquisitely tuned to the vibrant romantic colors, while at sixty or even seventy subtler shades predominate, much as the Purkinje Phenomenon of twilight hours mutes the bright reds and yellows to show us the more deeply nuanced tones of blue and green.

We can access the love that surrounds and suffuses us, but too often we remain blind to it, our senses perhaps overwhelmed and numbed by louder, more insistent inputs. So it is that many of us wander distracted in a stumbling search, groping and looking for something that eludes us, while the grail we seek we already possess: the ability to see, and more importantly, to feel.

And this, thru the incomparable generosity of The Giver, is what remains and what renews, from age to age and life to life.

𝓐𝓯𝓯ection

She is a small woman, not much over five feet. Hispanic, I would guess not Mexican but south of there. Guatemala perhaps, or if Mexico, some tiny village in the interior. Of her age I am uncertain; maybe forty-something, but my guess could be far afield. She works at a menial job in a restaurant, sweeping and mopping, cleaning the detritus of others' fast food. Where some might be lethargic and indifferent to the duties of such a job, she brings a serious mien and a quiet dignity to her work.

I visit this restaurant from time to time, usually alone; usually when I wish to be alone. I carry a book, a magazine, a newspaper – some article I want to read over lunch without distraction.

Sometime over the past few months this small woman came to notice me. Why, I cannot say. Sometimes, although not always, she will approach my table. She pauses in her work, looks at me directly, nods and in a soft voice says, "*Hello, sir.*"

I do not ignore her greeting, but respond in kind. She lingers a moment, then resumes her tasks, sweeping, mopping, bringing cleanliness and order to this busy place. I have not seen her speak to other customers.

Recently, because of travel and my own work responsibilities, I did not visit this restaurant for several weeks. When I returned, she again sought out my table and after her usual formal greeting she added, "*I miss you.*"

Her command of English is limited and does not include nuances of grammar. What she can say to me is constrained by this and by an innate reserve.

Last week I was back at the restaurant. Once again she approaches. "*Hello, sir,*" she says, "*How are you?*"

I look up from my reading and smile. "*I'm fine,*" I reply, "*How are you?*"

She nods to indicate she's OK. She holds my gaze a moment longer. "*God bless you, sir,*" she says.

I am startled by her benediction. "*Thank you – and you,*" my reply more mumbled than I would wish it.

The small woman moves on, resumes her sweeping, but I cannot return to my reading. Something here has touched me. When it comes time for me to leave I think perhaps I should ask the woman her name, introduce myself.

But I do not.

I do not exactly understand what is going on here. I am a 68-year-old man. I possess certain features and attributes that once occasioned a modicum of admiration from some females, but now I am . . . a 68-year-old man. Surely this small woman is not attracted to me in any sense remotely romantic, is she?

More likely, I think, it is not more than human being to human being. Perhaps I am alone in acknowledging that she is a person and not merely a broom or a mop. But why did she choose me to address?

I like this small woman. Not romantically, of course, but maybe because of the simple dignity she brings to her work and to our small and sporadic moments of interaction. She is, I think, a good woman.

A good person.

Or might she be perhaps an angel walking in our midst, solemnly sweeping up after us, blessing us with her presence?

My Semi-brilliant TV Debut

Mr. DeMille, I'm ready for my close up.
Gloria Swanson as Norma Desmond in <u>Sunset Boulevard</u>

Hard to imagine now, but in the late 50's television was the medium many believed would transform society for the better. Then in 1961 Newton Minnow, head of the FCC denounced it as a "vast wasteland" full of mindless fare, failing to live up to its potential. This kicked off a national debate: what the heck is TV for, anyway?

Sadly, but predictably, none of the debaters asked high school kids their opinion. We knew what TV was for. We'd have told them it was so we could run home after school to catch <u>The Little Rascals</u>, <u>The Many Loves of Dobie Gillis</u> or <u>American Bandstand</u>. We relied on Bandstand for valuable information on the latest pop hits. If Bob and Justine reckoned the new Everly Brothers number *"had a good beat, you could dance to it"* and gave it a 9, a zillion teens would zip out and plunk down a buck for a "45."

Ignoring the obvious truth of TV's real purpose, high-minded adults in DC and New York concluded that television could - and should - be used for education. These are the same folks who failed to notice that sales of those "Classic Comics" was minuscule compared to Archie, Superman or Porky Pig. Instead, the educational establishment grabbed hold of the notion kids might actually learn something from TV other than how to do The Stroll or the Chalypso. Educational TV was born.

St. Louis was not going to be left behind in this great transformation, nor was my small, inner city high school. Almost overnight, we found ourselves watching TV in the classroom. Not Bandstand, of course, but some boring documentary on Art in The Middle Ages or How Your Pancreas Works. The only advantage for us was that the teacher would have to turn out the lights so we could see TV, which made it easier to nap or pull your desk over and make out with the cute girl in the next row.

This was also how my friend Mitch and I found ourselves picked to represent McKinley High in a Jeopardy-style quiz show to be broadcast on the local PBS station. How it was determined we were the best candidates is puzzling, especially as the topic of the show was - The Federal Income Tax.

Nevertheless, we were *it* in this game and were sent off to meet with some CPA who was to bring us up to speed on tax law. How this particular CPA was chosen is also a mystery, but he lived way out in University City, which meant a long bus and streetcar ride with several transfers. And we didn't even get off school, but had to make the trip after. Missed Bandstand, which is probably why I'm still not great at The Mashed Potatoes.

We probably spent an hour or more with our tax tutor, who tried valiantly to explain taxable income, exemptions, deductions, FICA and tax brackets. I mean the guy really tried, but I'm pretty sure after the first thirty minutes he realized it was a lost cause and that he was working with a couple of guys who were destined years later to end up in the Pen for tax evasion, fraud or a host of other financial felonies.

The guy saw us to the door and after walking down the block I looked back and saw him wave while sadly shaking his head. As we walked to the bus stop, I asked Mitch if he'd understood any of what the guy'd tried to teach us.

"Not a word," he said.

"Me either."

Came the day of the show, the McKinley team was not overflowing with confidence as we entered the studio and found our assigned spots on the bleacher-type stand with the other 30 or so glum looking kids from all over St. Louis, none of whom had probably ever carried more than $5 in their wallet or purse but now represented the cream of the city's high school income tax expertise.

So, after some preliminaries, the torture began. The MC would call on some kid by name and high school, whereupon the poor schlub would have to stand and try gamely to answer some impossibly complex tax question. Miss and you were out. You'd have endure the humiliation of stumbling over your neighbor's feet to climb down off the bleachers.

There were a lot more misses than hits, so the bleachers thinned out rapidly. Mitch went down early. I envied him. Somehow, I kept guessing the right answers. I recall a couple of times I deliberately tried to give the wrong answer, only to have it turn out to be right. Finally, it was down to me and one other kid. Then, like an endlessly weary ping-pong game, the two of us kept at it back and forth, back and forth, until at long, l-o-o-o-o-n-g last I managed to guess wrong. Not sure how the other kid saw it, but it felt like a win to me.

Nielson didn't release a rating for the Income Tax Quiz show, nor did any critics review it. I expect it failed to garner a huge audience, as there was never another income tax quiz show on tv. Every one of my extended family had to watch, tho, as I'm certain did the families of the other contestants, younger members no doubt grudgingly. Likely the show's entire viewership.

Except.

I like to think our tutor tuned in as well, martini or Manhattan in hand and already fortified with several pre-show libations. "This should be wildly entertaining," I imagine him saying to himself, "In the same sense it would be enlightening to watch your entire life story shown not as a serious and flattering documentary but rather as a Road Runner cartoon where products of the Acme Anvil Company are continually dropped on your head from great heights by an annoying little bird who won't stop going 'Meep-meep.'"

Still, perhaps our tax teacher felt a little better about himself and his life's work when one of his proteges came *that close* to winning.

I don't know, maybe if I'd actually won the stupid quiz, I'd have gone on to be a famous tax attorney or something, made a ton of money and known how to shelter it in some offshore tax haven. 'Course then if the tax quiz show idea ever popped up again, I might find myself chosen to tutor a couple of high school kids who could give a shit less.

As it was, I didn't even get a little trophy or award for my 2nd place finish. On the other hand, maybe I learned a little something. By the time the internet came around I was pretty sure that wasn't gonna be the new medium that made everything better. Instead, it produced its own vast wasteland - social media. Also, I haven't gone to jail for tax fraud.

Yet.

Tom Kiske

Rain

A half-dark morning,

The sky dappled shades of gray.

An asphalt parking lot,

White lines a precise geometry,

Color only in ladies' umbrellas

As they scamper for refuge

From weather across rain-made streams

Meandering, imprisoned by no one's order

Or idea of what's right.

Rain, like all of nature

Is

And does

And offers neither explanation nor

Apology.

Fifty Years

Love's not Time's fool, though rosy lips and cheeks
Within his bending sickle's compass come . . .
Sonnet 116, William Shakespeare

Fifty years.

Fifty years of time. Calendar time, pages full of days, months flipped through then discarded for a new calendar, a new year. Clock time, ticking away the minutes and hours. Minutes and hours of our lives.

Some ancient peoples viewed time as a tangible force, governed and controlled by one of their panoply of gods.

Time is a thief. Jealously, he robs us of so much. Friends and classmates are stolen away. A spouse may be taken. Perverting the natural order of things, time may take one of our children, a soul-fracturing loss for which there is no recompense. Marriages fall victim to the dark invader against whom there is no defense. Little by little or in one sudden, voracious grab he takes our health or – worse – the health of one we hold dear.

Year by year he grows bolder, this Taker, and never is he satisfied. Vicious and uncaring, he steals what he will, leaving us only . . .. what?

Yes, Time does leave something behind for everything he takes, so perhaps he is less a thief than a masterful trader, albeit one who dictates his arbitrary terms and brooks no negotiation, no bargaining, no appeal.

What he leaves us in trade are our memories, a commodity that grows more precious with each tick of the clock, each page of the calendar. Like certain metals, memories seem to accrue a kind of patina over the years, a softly glowing layer that blurs hard edges, rendering them perhaps less true but far sweeter, far lovelier. So that they become not so much memories but dreams.

And if through all the years we have kept some friends of old, there is no finer use for memory's dreams than sharing them, like the lyrics to a well-known song best rendered in a harmony of complementing voices. The oldies but goodies. Like us.

Moments Without Function

Motion attracts attention. It's automatic, perhaps a survival mechanism. The eye registers movement, signals are sent to the brain, your head turns and the focus of your consciousness follows. You don't think about it, nor can you control it. A robot could be programmed to do the same.

Flowers bloom in the dappled morning sunlight outside the kitchen window. A tiny hummingbird comes by for breakfast and his helicoptering catches my eye. He prefers the lavender salvia to the white. So small he is, so fragile. Delicate as the blossoms at which he drinks, extracting from each a sip of nectar measurable in molecules.

Later, I'm walking from the car to the entrance of the fitness center. A light drizzle is falling. The clean, earthy smell of it (the "petrichor") arrests me. For a moment breathing is elevated from a mechanical act to sampling a rare delicacy. So good. So sweet.

Most of the time we function as machines, or as gears in some large machine. Walk, talk, eat, drink, work, sleep. When we break or wear out replacements are easily available. We're unplugged, removed, discarded. A new part is fitted in place. The machinery cranks on and we're forgotten.

But what of those silver moments? What of that mysterious chip inside each of us that finds enjoyment in the sight of a flitting hummingbird, that savors the merest hint of earthen perfume in an April rain? What nectar do we draw from such moments? What need is satisfied thereby; what mystic organ nourished?

Why are we fashioned with the capacity to appreciate, with the hunger to love and be loved? These functions - superfluous to the machine - what greater thing do they serve? And might that greater thing of rain-scent and hummingbird moments live on when the machine is no more than rust and dust?

𝓣exas 𝓘nsect 𝓛ore

Do you have Love Bugs where you are? We have Love Bugs where we are. Texas has lots of Love Bugs. We do not always have Love Bugs, but in Spring when we have Love Bugs, we have many, many Love Bugs. Some would say _too many. We'd be happy to export them by the bushel but there doesn't seem to be much of a market for Love Bugs. I expect there's a scientific name for the species - perhaps something taxonomic like Lovus Buggus. If so, it might create an inaccurate impression, as very few human persons hereabouts love us them buggusses.

So why are they called Love Bugs in the common parlance? It's because they "fly united" so to speak. It's a curious sight the first time you see a Love Bug. It looks like a chimerical creature with a head on both ends. Really, tho, you're observing two amorous Love Bugs of opposite "gender" rapturously replenishing their species. Evidently, they enjoy this immensely as they _always_ fly around that way. To my knowledge, no one has ever seen just one Love Bug. If any single Love Bugs exist, they're probably too embarrassed to show themselves in public. Evidence suggests you have to be a spectacularly ugly Love Bug boy not to - literally - hook up with a girlfriend.

Truthfully, tho, we merely presume these bugs are in love. It's possible they're simply overwhelmed with lust (maybe you remember what _that's_ like!). To date, science has been unable to penetrate into the psyche of these seemingly affectionate insects to determine the precise nature of their feelings for each other. It's far less challenging, however, to ascertain how most humans relate to the Love Bug.

We do not love the Love Bug.

We do not like the Love Bug.

"Despise' may not be too strong a word. Neither is "loathe."

Our disaffection is not a consequence of their proclivity for public displays of affection. By & large, Texans subscribe to The Isley Brothers' credo, "It's your thang, do what you wanna do." Of course our legislature is hell bent on modifying that for human-type people by adding a clause something like, "Except when it comes to public rest rooms, where you damn well better use the one corresponding to how your birth certificate characterizes your thang."

But getting back to the bugs, what makes them distasteful to actual persons of the human variety is their tendency for distracted flying. I mean, you can understand how splitting the limited focus of their itty-bitty brains between flying and uh, *reproducing* would be problematic, but you'd think that over a hundred years or so evolution would've provided a mechanism whereby Love Bugs would avoid public thoroughfares.

If you thought that, though, you'd be wrong. There's ample evidence of this evolutionary oversight because for a few weeks each Spring, Texas drivers unwillingly become amateur entomologists. We're aided in this avocation by the chemical composition of the Love Bug body. Unlike the human body which is 60% water, Love Bugs are 90% glue. For this reason, even a short drive during the Love Bugs' Season of Love results in an impressive, semi-permanent collection of their sticky carcasses displayed across your windshield and pretty much the entire front end of your car, truck or SUV. If you ride a motorcycle, your face is the pallet for Love Bugs' suicidal art exhibit. This is why knowledgeable motorcyclists don't smile while riding.

While normally the mass suicide of a significant percentage of the population of any species would be an occasion of angst, in this case it's understandable if your emotional reaction is not sadness, pity and grief, but rather, "Ewwww!" Especially because depending on the total mass of Love Bug corpses arrayed on your vehicle and their state of decay, they freakin' STINK!

When you think about it, tho, maybe for the Love Bug it's not such a bad way to end a brief existence. Whether love or mere lust, to be instantaneously extinguished at a, well, *climatic* moment might be the best any of us can hope for.

Say what you will about the Love Bugs, they come and they go.

Tom Kiske

A Poetry not in Words

There is a poetry different from words
More than words.
You can awaken to it
In the strangest way:
Late afternoon, Saturday, on your back
porch
You see it
Beyond the fence and forest
The many shaded greens.
At the top the trees sway
Under His hand
With such stirring grace
It lifts my earthbound eyes,
Lifts the deep knowing upward
And shows in easy movement
What all hearts know
But seldom speak.

Poems stir and flow
And whisper
Like treetops,
Reaching higher
Into Him.

The Mississippi

The mighty river. The place-keeper. The unmoved mover. I am his son and revere him still. He was there and is there and will be there. I know him, far more than that Other One, that One cloistered in His stubborn silence.

The Father of Waters keeps his mysteries too, hidden in his murky, unexplored depths, but his face at least he shows me and if his murmuring voice answers no great questions, it hints of something close to the eternal and grants a solemn calm, a peace that needs no cathedral, no obeisance.

Perhaps more than the Other One, the Mississippi swallows up our sins and carries them away, giving us back that which sustains us, water to our thirst. He makes no claim of power or wisdom beyond what he shows us, nor does he demand ritual or worship.

He simply *is,* and perhaps his mere being is a reminder, in the face of our artificial complexities, to also simply *be.*

Learning, Forgetting

"...what does the forest do Monday through Friday?
I was a boy; I knew; now I have forgotten..."
"Clerk's Song II, by Norman H. Russell in <u>Voices from Wah-
Kon-Tah</u>, Dodge & McCullough

It's twilight and I'm wondering: is life a journey of learning or forgetting? For a city boy like me, it's not about forests but about first times. There's only one first time for each thing: one first car, one first kiss, one first ... you will understand.

To thrill to things. To have that uncertain, unsettling feeling that centers in your stomach. It's the realm of butterflies and fantasies, where we test ourselves and learn the limits of our being. The lesson is often misunderstood. We remember the limit, forgetting the wonder of the test. We seek safety and contentment and in the search for those beguiling twins, find ourselves lost on a bland and featureless plain that stretches endlessly before us. We've been here so long. Too long. There is no threat, no danger. We've learned risk avoidance well; so well it's hard to recall the early times, whence we came and where we though we once were destined to go.

There was a time everything was new and the great blue sky beckoned high and wide before me. Before I learned laziness was sinful there were foolish hours I lie on my back and watched clouds drifting past, aimless as me, without care, as majestic and serene as me. One summer afternoon I reached out to the sky with a kite fashioned by my own hand and flew it high, to the limit of the tether in my earthbound hand, then set it free to soar on alone as I flew with it in my unschooled mind. No experimenting Ben Franklin, I, yet a lesson was learned that comes back to me across the years. It is a Primer not in words or pages, but in feelings inscribed indelibly on my journal heart.

I am a St. Louis boy a thousand miles from home, but still from and of the old red brick city at the confluence of mighty rivers that flow through me and bind me to the place of my boyhood. It is my jugular and my connection to the mystic pulse whose beat is measured in cadences far greater than the clock that counts away my brief hours. Before I was, it was, and it will remain when I am dust. For a moment I sat and marveled at its muddy sinews and I was part of its timeless rhythm - this inland sea, this Huckleberry harbinger, this Meriwether compass – in its irresistible flood and flow and tide.

This is a hand-made brick city at its heart and here is where the warmth and strength are found. Walking these ancient streets, my soles touch stones how many trod before and wore down a millimeter awaiting me? There's geologic comfort here that counterposes fresh green leaves of Spring and youth and tender young love. It has been done by others before me, but now, this time, it is for me.

There were lips before, but none like hers; no mouth so sweet. There was perfumed hair, but not like this. It couldn't be. Never a smile like hers, nor skin so soft and pliant. Lovers strolled these lanes, I'm certain, but none had such thoughts as ours, nor did music ever cure the air as our sweet songs do. I hear them still.

And yet it goes away. I have my work, which won't relent. I have my duties and responsibilities that won't let up. The alarm rings early and I must rise. It's time to go – forget those carefree days. Forget. Mortgage payment's due and Mastercard demands what coinage remains. They collect and cannot hear my repentant cry, nor is there caring in these conversations. What has become of what once was me? Where is that shy and sleepy boy? Is it too late to wake him?

But he's there, whispering his presence. Like stars and trees and mountains, there is nothing I must do. I am, as He once taught, what I am. And under all, through all, above all, is but love – splendorous and supreme.

Is it only in those final fleeting moments I might at length learn what once I knew and have forgot and forgot again? Am going further, to some rare and nameless range I've never seen or known?

Or am I going home?

In the Slipstream

"Get your motor runnin'
Head out on the highway
Looking for adventure
In whatever comes our way."
Born to be Wild, Steppenwolf

1963. It would be a late Spring Break trip for four south St. Louis guys a couple of years out of high school. Nowadays kids go all over the globe. Back then none of us had ever been out of Missouri. There was only one place we wanted to go: Fort Lauderdale. We'd heard Connie Francis sing "Where the Boys Are" in the movie, salivated over Yvette Mimieux in her bikini, marveled at Annette Funicello's transformation from Mouseketeer to Beach Party babe, dreamed of going Surfin' USA with The Beach Boys, maybe hooking up with a Little Surfer Girl. Yeah, where the boys were had to also be where the girls were and everybody knew that was in the sunshine state, in Fort Lauderdale.

It began as only a dream, a fantasy, an idea we played with knowing it wasn't possible because we had a big problem: no car. No car, no trip, no surfer girls.

But then one day, a miracle. Mike announced, "I can get us a car." He was serious. How he managed to pull it off none of us knew, but it didn't matter. The sun burst thru the clouds, flowers bloomed and all was right with the world. We had wheels - that's what mattered!

A few days later, Mike picked us each up and we saw for the first time our mode of transportation: a ten- or twelve-year-old turtle-back Pontiac straight 8, muddy green in color. Back then a new car might be good for 5 or 6 years, maybe 65,000 miles. Did we check the odometer, the tread on the tires, the dipstick? Did we ask about insurance coverage? Ha. We tossed our gear in the trunk and hit the road, St. Louis to somewhere in Florida, where the girls were.

We were not obsessed with planning. A few bucks in our pockets, swim suits, underwear and a change of clothes in our duffels and, I think, a map and we were set. The interstate highway system was still being built at the time, so most of the way we were on old blacktop roads, some four lanes, more two. We figured we'd share time behind the wheel so we could drive straight thru with no intermediate overnights. We made it to Alabama without incident, but then fatigue began to take a toll. In the dark of night, we found ourselves on a fine, broad highway, maybe a finished part of the interstate system, and we kept seeing exit signs for Dothan. Every few miles, we'd see "Dothan 3 miles" plus an arrow pointing left. Kept seeing them. Dothan never got closer, never got farther. Always 3 miles.

"Man," Bill commented, "that's gotta be the longest town in America."

Then we started noticing a Chevy dealership we'd seen before. The third time we saw the same thing we finally realized we were on a loop, a circumferential highway circling Dothan, Alabama!

There was no argument when someone suggested we were getting loopy ourselves and it was time for a break. We pulled into the next roadside diner we came across. I don't know what time it was, but coffee and pancakes hit the spot. Refueled, our confidence unshaken by the slight navigation error, we were back on the road, found our way off the Dothan circle and headed south once again.

Things were going pretty well and we let out a collective cheer when we crossed the state line into Florida. Minutes later we weren't so happy. We weren't happy at all. On a little two-lane blacktop in the wee hours without another vehicle - or anything else - in sight, the Green Machine "failed to proceed." I may have been driving because I remember the gas pedal revved the engine ok, but the car wasn't responding. What the heck?!

We coasted to a stop mostly on the shoulder and looked at each other. It was quiet in the car and outside, except for the sound of giant Florida mosquitos hitting the windows. I mean giant mosquitoes. This doesn't seem possible now, but in my memory the

Kamikaze blood-suckers actually rocked the car when they self-destructed.

Now what do we do? No cell phones in 1963, no calling AAA. I think Warren popped the hood and scratched his head. Then we started pushing. Pushing and swatting mosquitos. I'm not sure how far we pushed the heavy Pontiac, but we finally made it to a little town. Marianna Florida.

This is where my memory gets kinda vague. What I think happened is we left the car in the parking lot of some mechanic's garage and walked further on to this little motel. I know we ended up in the motel, all four of us sharing a room. Exactly how we got there is less clear.

What is clear is that one of us was looking out the window when a late model Buick pulled in to the motel. A man and woman got out, a young girl maybe 12 or 13 followed, then two older girls. Girls! A tall blonde and a shorter brunette, both about our age. They all toted luggage into their room and then in a short while, our lookout turned back to us.

"The girls are going to the pool," he announced excitedly.

Well, never, never-ever did four guys get into swim trunks as quickly as we did. Then we casually, coolly sauntered up to the little motel swimming pool.

The girls pretended to ignore us. We pretended to ignore them. For a while. Then somebody broke the ice - I don't remember who - and pretty soon we were all friends, chatting and laughing and, well, flirting. It was a Goldilocks night, not too hot, not too cold. Just right. The water in the pool sparkled and shimmered and I swear there was the hint of some sweet Southern fragrance in the air although that might've just been my imagination. It was the kind of night that only happens when you're young, when time is a bottomless well you're sure you can drink from forever, all that lies ahead is fun and possibility and nothing will ever go wrong or sour.

Best of all, I thought the blonde maybe kinda liked me. Mike made some moves on the brunette, but too soon the girls said they needed to head back inside. We walked them to their car where they needed something out of the trunk. When they retrieved whatever it was, Bill slammed the trunk lid closed.

Then the blonde - *my* girl - innocently asked, "Uh, who has the keys?"

Uh-oh. Bill's face turned pale as we stood staring at the closed, locked trunk.

Warren, our car guy, had an idea. "Sometimes," he said, "On GM cars you can pop the trunk by pulling on the side fins."

The automotive tail fin fad was already waning by '63, but the Buick still had vestigial ones so we lined up on each side and pulled. Pulled hard. Then pulled again. And one more time.

Nothing.

Uh. Hmmm.

Then the blonde, with a devilish grin, dangled the keys from her fingertips. It was exactly the kind of prank the four of us guys might've pulled, but this girl pulled it on us. For some reason it made me smile.

Because we were all friends now, before we said goodnight, we made arrangements to meet in a few days at the Sunken Gardens in St. Petersburg.

Yeah, not bad for our first night in Florida, but the next morning we had a major problem to solve. Got dressed and walked back to the garage where we'd left the Green Machine.

"Bad news," the mechanic said, "Your transmission's outta fluid and burned up. Needs a major rebuild. It'll run ya around $300."

Three hundred bucks? The four of us together didn't have anywhere near that. I doubt any of us had ever even seen that amount of cash. What could we do?

Here's where it paid to have a car guy in our group. "How much just to fill the transmission," Warren asked.

"20 bucks," the mechanic said, "but I don't . . ."

"Fill it up."

We trusted Warren a lot more than some mechanic in Marianna, Florida.

By the time we drove back to the motel the Buick and the girls were gone. We checked out and headed to St. Pete. The car seemed to run OK altho there was a lingering burnt or burning odor that was a bit unsettling.

We made it to our scheduled meeting with the motel girls and spent most of the day with them on the beach. Never found suitable companions for Warren and Bill, tho and so the next day we swung around and headed back up the peninsula because Warren insisted he had to stop by and visit relatives in Silver Spring or Silver Lake or something. It was probably how he justified the trip to his mom and dad.

From there we continued up the east coast, stopping in St. Augustine to visit one of the historic forts the city's proud of. I don't recall which one we saw, but we did take a few pictures to prove we were interested in history and hadn't just come to Florida for the, uh, wildlife. Looking at the pictures today I see a road-weary crew not happy to be on the return leg of our odyssey.

The way back to St. Louis took us along many of the same two-lane highways we'd traveled in the opposite direction only a few days before. Much of the time we were driving at night. When it was Warren's turn, I thought he drove too fast, out-driving the headlights, but when I took over, I naturally had to prove he wasn't the only one who could top the speed limit even in the dark on twisting turns, up and down hills. Even S-curves.

Then one of us came up with the brilliant idea we could save gas by slip-streaming an 18-wheeler. We'd seen it in Formula 1 races. Also called drafting, you get really close to the car ahead of you so you reduce your wind resistance. There's almost a partial vacuum and you're actually pulled ahead by the car in front. We figured it would work even better if we slip streamed a big rig.

The downside is you have to get really close, like maybe 5 feet or less. It works, though; you can let up on the gas and not slow down. You can't do it very long because air flow thru your radiator is reduced. The temperature gauge goes up quickly. The other thing is that it's incredibly dangerous, not to mention dumb. If the truck slows suddenly, you have virtually zero reaction time. We did it, though, Warren and I both. We got lucky and survived. Made it back to St. Louis without incident or accident. The transmission held up fine although that burnt smell was with us the whole way.

Years later I realized that for that whole time of our lives we'd been traveling in the slip stream of time, part of a youthful culture held together by rock 'n roll, dumb movies and the illusion of our own invulnerability. By the end of 1963 the youthful American President would be dead by an assassin's hand and his successor would lead us into the muddy, bloody nightmare of Vietnam, ripping our nation asunder, creating rifts and wounds yet to fully heal.

But the roads we took to Florida and back held no hint of the dark days around the bend. Instead, we were blissfully, innocently pulled forward by a vague dream that somewhere down the road a pretty girl might smile at us and actually like us. *Really* like us.

And a pretty girl did.

My Dam

I'm trying to build a beaver dam
Athwart the quickening current
of my personal tributary
That feeds the great, earth-circling river
Of yesterdays.

Stories are the twigs,
Dark mud the mortar of lost remembrance
And secret sins.

I know my task is futile
for I hear the rapids' warning -
The flood is coming soon
To flush away my fragile, fanciful work,
carrying but dumb debris to the delta
and beyond.

But maybe someone someday passing here
might recall, dimly along their journey
That here a little pond once was
where time found respite and rested
in silver silence,
Smiling at the ancient sun.

𝕵𝖆𝖈𝖐'𝖘 𝕯𝖎𝖑𝖊𝖒𝖒𝖆

Jack did not want to make the call. It was embarrassing and too many embarrassments had already befallen him in his young life. He put it off for a day and then a couple of days and then a week. He hoped it might just go away, but of course it didn't. Then the decomposition began in earnest and the stench grew worse and worse until the problem could no longer be ignored.

He wasn't even sure who to call. It was such an unusual thing, and so *big.* Jack's goal, of course, was simply to get rid of the thing. The less fuss the better. No questions, no inquiry, no publicity. Just haul it off. It was purely a disposal problem, and that was how he described it to the trash hauler. Midway through the phone conversation, though, he realized he's blown it. He was too anxious, too nervous, and the man had picked up on that, became suspicious.

"What kind trash you got there?" the guy asked.

"Well, uh, it's kinda hard to describe, but we definitely don't need it or want it anymore."

"Not toxic, is it?" the man went on, "Because that would take special handling. We're not equipped for that sort of thing."

"No, no," Jack stammered, "I don't think you'd consider it toxic. It is rather large, though."

"How large?" the man demanded.

"Quite large."

"Like what? The size of a horse?"

"Oh, at least."

"At least? Listen, it's not organic waste is it? I mean like animal or something."

Well, that was that. Jack couldn't *lie* to the fellow. Anyway, as soon as they showed up, they'd have seen for themselves what it was. Nope, the trash men were not going to be of help. Before hanging up, the man suggested calling the local SPCA, but Jack knew that would prove equally unproductive.

Still, he did not want to make the call he knew he should make and so he procrastinated another two days, hoping another solution might make itself evident. The only thing that became evident, though, was that the smell was getting worse. Much worse. And then there were the flies. Flies were becoming a big problem. All that buzzing about. They were everywhere, even getting inside the house. It was most unpleasant, but at least Jack lived in a rural area, so there were no neighbors to complain about the nuisance.

Finally, after bracing himself with a strong shot of whiskey, Jack dialed 9-1-1.

"What's the nature of your emergency?" she asked.

"There is," Jack gulped, "a giant in my backyard."

"I beg your pardon?"

Jack reconsidered his phrasing. "There's a very large person out back of my house."

"Uh-huh. Is this person threatening you?"

"Well, not anymore. He's dead, you see."

There's a dead person in your yard, sir?"

"Yes," Jack answered, growing somewhat more assertive as the whiskey kicked in. "A really, really *big* dead person."

"And how did this person die?"

"He fell," Jack managed, "He fell from a great height and the fall killed him."

"I see." said the operator, "What exactly did he fall from?"

Jack thought for a moment before he answered. "A plant," he said at last.

"The man died falling from a plant?" the operator asked incredulously.

"Well, you have to understand it was quite a tall plant."

"Like a tree?" The operator suggested.

"No, not really. More like a ... a ... uh ..."

"Yes?"

"OK, a *stalk*," Jack said

"He fell off a stalk?"

"Yes. Specifically, a bean stalk."

The 9-1-1 operator hung up. Jack couldn't blame her. He knew it sounded crazy, sounded like a prank call. If someone had called Jack with that story, he'd have thought they were crazy. But Jack was pretty sure he wasn't crazy. A little naïve, perhaps, maybe a little greedy, but not crazy. He wasn't imagining this. That think was *out there*!

It was out there and it stunk. Jack knew he had no other choice. He re-dialed the emergency number and the same operator answered.

"Don't hang up." Jack said quickly, "I'm not making this up. There's this dead guy in my yard and somebody's gotta do something!"

"Alright, sir, give me your full name and address."

Jack complied dutifully.

"Wait a minute," the operator said, "that sounds familiar."

"Crap!" Jack thought.

"Yeah, weren't we out there not too long ago?"

"Uh, maybe."

"Now I remember. Somebody was injured. Was that you?"

"Well, that was actually quite a while ago."

"Yes, yes," the operator continued, "it's coming back to me. It was you and a female, right?"

"Really," Jack said, "Can't we discuss that some other time?"

"The two of you'd gone off somewhere. Climbed a hill or something. You had some cockamamie story then, too. Said you'd gone up to – ha-ha – fetch a pail of water. Then you sustained some injury, if I'm not mistaken."

"Uh-huh, but getting back to the problem at hand ..."

"Your head." the operator said. "You'd broken ..."

"Alright, already," Jack exclaimed, "I fell down and broke my crown! Are you happy now?"

"And the girl ..."

"Jill."

"Yes, that was her name. She ..."

"She came tumbling after." Jack said, "It was in all the papers. On the TV news. Made my life quite miserable. Thank you so much for bringing that up."

"Sorry, sir, it's just that, well, with the head injury and now this thing with giants ..."

"Listen," Jack said in a last gamble, "It's not appropriate to call 'em giants any more."

"How's that?"

"Well, it's impolite. They prefer 'large persons' or 'the ample of stature. Really isn't nice to make fun of them, is it?"

"Oh, no, sir," the operator mumbled apologetically, "and that was certainly not my intent."

"Then do you suppose we might possibly get someone out here to deal with this problem?"

"Yes, sir. Right away. Can you hold a sec?"

Jack didn't want to hold, but the operator had a quick switchboard trigger finger and before he could object, he was listening to Barry Manilow over the phone and hoping he wasn't going to have to go through the same irritating conversation with whomever the operator put him through to. He needn't have worried. The next voice on the line was a familiar one.

"Uh, sir?" the operator began.

"Yes, yes, is someone coming out?"

"Well, not exactly. I spoke with Public Works and they said they'd be happy to dispose of any, like, animal remains, but that giants ... er, large persons, were not their bailiwick."

"Can't you get the sheriff or police or whatever to come?

"Tried. They both said unless there was a crime they couldn't respond."

"Fire Department?"

"Not unless he's on fire or stuck in a tree."

"City Council?"

"Does the large gentleman vote?"

"Coroner?"

"On vacation."

"Dog catcher, for chrissake?"

"Now, sir, there's no call for that kind of talk. Besides, I think you know the answer."

"Yeah," Jack muttered wearily, "Unless he's barking or biting someone, they can't be troubled, right?"

"I'm afraid so, sir. I've tried every city department I can think of. Maybe you should call the state offices."

"Sure," Jack barked, "Why don't I just pop over to the governor's office and see if he's in the mood to carve up this huge freakin' carcass himself. Make a nice stew for the missus and kiddies, hey?"

"Uh, well, my shift is over now, sir. Goodbye and thank you for calling 9-1-1. Have a nice day."

Jack stared at the silent receiver for a long time, shaking his head and cursing under his breath. Finally hanging up, he reached for the bottle. It was cheap whiskey and it burned all the way down his throat. The bitterness and pain matched his mood and he reflexively took another greedy guzzle. He could feel the alcohol percolating up to his troubled brain. The room began to dim and spin. That was when he heard the high-pitched voice.

"Shoulda left us where ya found us, shouldn't ya?"

"Wha-a-a ..." Jack slurred, "Who's there?"

"Just me, one of your stolen treasures," the voice went on, "you *thief*."

Jack looked around, finally spotting the source of the accusation sitting on the table next to him.

"You!" Jack yelled, "Damn little harp. If it hadn't have been for you, I wouldn't be in this pickle."

"Oh, my fault, is it?" the harp replied, "All I did was try to keep you from stealing me from my master."

"Yeah?" Jack shouted, "Well, I'm your master now, and you gotta do what I say."

"Yes, master," the little harp sneered sarcastically.

"Well, then, *play!*" Jack commanded.

And sure enough, the harp began playing – the very same Barry Manilow song Jack had been forced to listen to when he was put on hold by the 9-1-1 operator. Only the harp was singing along, and singing badly. As everyone knows, the only thing worse than a Barry Manilow number is a *bad* Barry Manilow number. Moreover, Jack knew it was bad on purpose.

"I'll teach you!" Jack screamed, grabbing the harp and flinging it with all his might against the cottage wall.

The harp shattered on impact. The frame broke in two, most of the strings parting and flying off with an ear-piercing din of "sproings" and "poiks" and "wangwangs."

But the little harp didn't stop playing. Really, it couldn't, because in his anger, Jack had neglected to *tell* it to stop. And the only thing worse than a bad Barry Manilow number is a bad Barry Manilow played badly by a busted-up harp with a bunch of busted strings. Especially when the harp hates its new master.

"La-la-la-sproing." went the harp, "Poingity-thonk-wheeeng-doink."

"Aarrrghhh," Jack screamed, clapping his hands over his ears, "Lemme outta here!"

He jumped up from the chair and ran crazily through the cottage, heading for the door and the relative quiet and darkness beyond. As he passed the kitchen table, the hen Jack had swiped from the giant laid another iron pyrite egg, which rolled onto the floor under Jack's left foot, causing him to lose his balance, fall heavily onto the stone floor and break, once again, his crown.

"Later, Jack groggily regained consciousness on a stretcher as the paramedics were carrying him out the door, over the walkway to the ambulance waiting by the curb. As he passed by, Jack noticed an oddly familiar little fellow standing beside the pathway.

"Beans?" the man smiled and asked, "Can I interest you in some magic beans, young man?"

It took all the strength of all the paramedics to restrain Jack and wrestle him shrieking incoherently into the emergency vehicle.

And thus it came to pass that the state finally did help poor Jack in a way, for he was carted off to the state hospital for the seriously wacky, where he underwent many years of psychotherapy, and although he became quite skilled at knitting, making beaded bracelets and other craft activities, he never overcame his phobic aversion to beans and harps and Barry Manilow music, and he never returned to his little cottage, where, it is said, on certain moonlit nights, you can still her soft, plaintive notes from a little harp whose heart, as well as whose frame and strings, were broken by a foolish young man called, simply, Jack.

But what of the giant? Did he truly exist or was he merely the product of an unfortunate young fellow's "broken crown?"

No-one knows for sure, but there is an old woman in that part of the country who lives, together with all her children (and she has so many she doesn't know what to do) in an oddly shaped house that resembles nothing more closely than a very large – you might almost say a giant-sized – shoe.

Secret Lives

We all have secret lives
That dwell so deep within
And would come out
And would give in
If only wishes were
And only wonders might
And things we thought
Could never be
Would be for but one night.

But lives that hide their face inside
Won't speak, nor see
The light of morn,
And champions whose strength
Could ne'er be beat
Will never yet be born.

For all that we could see
Or dream
Is but tomorrow's child,
And truth will never show to me
What flowers in the wild
By paths my feet will never tread
In lands foreign and far,
'Neath suns whose light will never dawn
And nights without a star.

A Brief Discourse

Alright, class, today's topic is:

Peace of Mind

and the quest to attain it. Anyone have any thoughts? Epicurus, how 'bout you?

Sir, I believe peace of mind lies in understanding the true nature of things and then aligning one's living in conformity to that nature.

Shows thought, Epi, but what is the true nature of things?

Well, uh . . ..

What about you Stoic fellas – how do you think peace of mind can be achieved?

Easy, sir, just abjure all passions, all longings, that sort of thing.

That might work, but wouldn't it be a rather insipid way to live?

Why you smart-ass mother . . ..!

Easy, Action – no passions, remember? Maybe the Jesus freaks have an idea.

Bless you, Professor. We hold that faith is the answer, but really, true peace of mind is for the next life. Up in the clouds, you know, wearing a golden halo and strumming a harp. Harp music's real relaxing, right? Unless some joker requests "Louie, Louie,"

Sorry, boys, that sounds like your typical mystic mythology and leaves us kinda hopeless down here on planet Earth.

Well, peace be with you anyway, dear, kindly old Professor.

Who's that in the back row with his hand up? That you, Thomas?

Yes, sir. I know I'm just a kid from South St. Louis and not anywhere near as smart as them other fellas, but I do keep a journal and you know what? Sometimes – not always, but sometimes – I feel a certain peace of mind writing in it.

Not bad, young man. A good empirical approach. Anything further?

Well, yes sir. I'm not sure it's appropriate to mention here, especially in from of them Christians, but I've got this girlfriend, Margie, see, and when we finish fu . . . er, doin' the dirty deed, if you catch my drift, I feel pretty damn peaceful.

Hmmm. You find peace with a piece. Interesting. That may have some merit despite your explanation having caused seizures among the Christians, driving poor Margie from the classroom in tears and making everyone blush thru their grins. I may have to do some personal experimentation to test your approach.

Be sure to wear a condom, Professor!

𝔇eregulate the 𝔖uperbowl

We're in the midst of a flurry of deregulation, with the President promising to remove 75% of all government regulations, a program Congress is spearheading by ridding us of the rule against dumping coal mine tailings into creeks and the provision that subjects folks with mental problems to a few questions before they can buy a gun. Perhaps this is the ideal time to also look into the burdensome regulations that stifle sporting events.

The NFL, for example, has over 60 rules for which a team can be penalized. That's obviously way too many and likely the reason viewership is down. Let's pare them back. Surely the Superbowl would be far more entertaining without that arbitrary rule a team can only have 11 players on the field or that you only get four downs. That's a bad deal and needs to be renegotiated. Likewise, those silly prohibitions against face-masking, pass interference, holding, clipping, the chop block & roughing the passer or kicker. Football players aren't sissies. Let them play! Get rid of half the officials. One referee, that's plenty. First and ten? Who said it has to be ten? Let's open up the game - and the country - to some real competition and make everything great again.

Rules? We don't need no stinking rules!

The Global Gravity Shift

Global warming remains controversial in some circles despite convincing evidence the climate is getting hotter. Meanwhile, as scientists and politicians debate the issue an equally momentous change seems to be underway that's apparent to most ordinary folks but which to date has escaped scientific scrutiny.

Things are getting heavier. Me, for example. In the past my personal weight seemed linked to the decade. In the sixties I weighed in at 160 or so. In the seventies, I ratchetted up to the mid-170's but still took some pride in being able to wear my dad's 32" leather WWII Marine Corps belt. I probably pushed over the 180 mark in the eighties, but then lost track in the ensuing decade. Maybe I hit 190 although I prefer to believe otherwise.

I think the trouble started with the new millennium. The link was broken. Obviously, there was no way to tie an adult's weight to the 00's and so the whole thing broke down. With no controls in place, gravity started accumulating, throwing our system of weights and measures into a cocked hat. Everything is just getting heavier and heavier. And there's nothing the ordinary joe can do about it. You starve yourself, work out like crazy and the next day you get on the bathroom scale and you're UP a pound!

Does that make any sense?

Of course not. It's got to be that the pull of gravity is getting stronger.

For further evidence you needn't go any farther than the gym. Ten years ago, I could easily curl 120 pounds. Now I'm lucky to do 110 on a good day. Skip a week, gravity gains on me and I struggle with 105.

It's the Global Gravity Shift and it's frightening. How do you account for this phenomenon? What's the cause? Is this weight gain manmade, possibly the result of fracking? Maybe it's those carbon emissions or ozone or something. Maybe the air's gotten heavier and is pushing down on us more. I don't think it's soft drinks. I mean, they're *soft*, right? And a quarter-pounder couldn't make that much difference, could it? Even with cheese?

Nah.

Sooner or later professional science-type guys will look into the problem and figure it out for us. Meanwhile, I'm thinking we should just re-calibrate our scales and stuff. If we could make, say, 185 the new 160, I'd sure feel a lot better about myself.

Reason Creek

4:02 a.m.

I leave my driveway. The road is empty at this hour. Highway 6 stretches before me in rolling sections defined by the reach of the Toyota's headlights. A long drive through the darkness looms ahead.

Some distance down the road I cross a small stream. Breason Creek, the sign says. For a moment I read it as Reason Creek. I am awake but not yet fully wakeful. It is not hard to think I may have crossed some important border, entered some sinister, unmapped region, a murky, treacherous terrain fraught with perils seen and unseen. The night shifts things. The road is less familiar. Unremembered curves and dips appear. Is this the route to the Med Center or am I driving an endless highway that winds and twists, rises abruptly and falls precipitously, goes on and on and on through a desolate landscape but leads nowhere but despair?

A pair of red lights ahead become malevolent eyes watching for their chance. The witchy wind moves and objects scurry along the shoulder of the road at the periphery of my vision - objects that might be nothing more than a drifting plastic bag, or might be ghastly hounds let loose from Below to feed on the unwary traveler.

Somewhere along this stretch last week two college students' lives ended in an early morning head-on arranged by alcohol or demons or both. Do the detached spirits of these kids still wander the lonesome road, confused and frightened, searching desperately for their once-bright futures, snuffed out in an instant and now forever, irretrievably lost?

Overhead, a half-moon creeps tentatively from behind scudding clouds, then ducks timidly back, leaving the countryside blacker than before.

Thousands of years ago early humans gathered around campfires lit as much, I think, to keep the night at bay as to provide warmth. Exploring the new tool of language, they shared tales of their own imaginings, conjuring gods and devils to explain what was beyond their understanding, to assure themselves that the world was ordered and not random, not mere chaos. Fear must be reined in, can be permitted only a limited dominion.

In the same way, my five-year-old grandson wants his bedtime stories scary, but not *too* scary. We "suspend disbelief" to enjoy the shiver of supernatural creatures, of inexplicable happenings, but it is a temporary condition voluntarily entered into within the context of solid rationality. Suspended disbelief cannot be allowed to swell into actual belief and acceptance, lest we plummet over the edge into a bottomless abyss that admits of no escape. This, not the Eden fable, is the true Fall.

When we cross the boundary and leave behind the realm of reason, we find vast forces arrayed against us, the gaping maw of ignorance slathering in the night, mindlessly snapping at anything within reach, seeking to satisfy its terrible, insatiable hunger, crying out to devour the light - *hating* the light its eyes can never see.

Mankind was long enslaved in the Outer Darkness and still today there are those who portray the chains of unreason, the shackles of unbridled passions, the iron mask of avarice, as comforts denied us by logical thought. The voices of those who tempt us to abandon our single weapon against indenture to The Beast are loud and persistent, and it is in dark and lonely nights we are most vulnerable to their deceptive allure.

But our way is the way of light. The road is long and the travel is often hard. We are on the right path. A bright destination lies ahead.

We must not turn back.

Just Do Your Best

When I was a child, many times I faced a challenge I feared I'd be unable to master. Whether it was a looming exam in school, something related to sports, a social event or any of the host of unfamiliar and thus frightening tests that regularly spring up in the bewildering world of childhood, I would worry myself into a state of near panic as the date for the encounter drew ever nearer. "What if I can't do this" would shift to "I don't think I can do this," and finally, "I can't do this."

I was a boy and boys are expected to face up to whatever life throws at them. Boys should be strong. Boys never, *ever* disappoint their fathers or fail to measure up to whatever standard they imagine Dad has set. I could not confess my anxieties to my father.

So, when the fear could no longer be contained, it was my mother to whom I turned. She would listen sympathetically, murmur "Uh-huh" and nod. Sometimes she had a valuable tip or suggestion to offer. More often, though, once I'd talked myself out her advice was simple and universally applicable, no matter what specific problem I was wrestling with. "Just do your best," she'd say, "An angel can do no more."

I don't know where she learned those words. Maybe from her mother. Maybe something she read. Or maybe an angel whispered them in her ear. I only know those few words never failed to comfort me. The phrase seemed to lift the burden of expectations from my shoulders. I had only a vague notion of what an angel might be like, but clearly, they were celestial beings, presumably close to God and thus no doubt imbued with vast power. A lot more power than me. But even the sword-wielding Archangel Michael could only "do his best." Same as me.

My mother's simple wisdom carried me thru many trials and tribulations.

But after high school I went away to college and confronted with challenges an order of magnitude more difficult and intense than ever before, I lost track of the formula for keeping it all in perspective. I lost track for a long and often dark time. As time went on my life grew more complex, my responsibilities far larger and more crucial than ever I'd imagined. As a grown man my nights were often sleepless, troubled with self-doubt and the same "What if I can't" worries that plagued me as a boy.

Until one Father's Day my boy gave me a very special gift, something he'd made himself, at school or in Scouts. It was a figure made from a clothespin; a face painted on the knob-like top. It was embedded in a plaster base & its arms were pipe cleaners, bent in such a way they carried a small card, no more than an inch square. The message printed on the card was "Do your best."

Simple, comforting words come 'round again thru my son. Maybe angels know when their message is needed.

That figure sat on my desk thru-out the remainder of my career, a constant and comforting reminder that whatever task I faced could not demand perfection nor even success, only that I try, that I do my best. After all, an angel can do no more.

Long after I reached semi-retirement a small group of old school friends - my best and closest friends - had a mini-reunion of sorts. There was an open-ended "homework assignment" in preparation for the get-together. The instructions were simple: bring something that's important to you. Some brought their college diploma or some plaque, trophy or award they'd won.

I brought a clothespin figure in a plaster base.

At the Intersection

November 12, 2014, 5:30 a.m. I'm sitting in the pred-dawn darkness at Cambridge and Fannin, the heart of Houston's Medical Center, a short distance from the destination that's had me on the road since just after four. I'm listening to "All Day Music" on the car radio, waiting for the traffic signal. One of the Metro light rail trains whizzes past, lit up from inside. More automobile traffic than you might imagine at this hour. A few pedestrians, bundled up against the cold front that blew in yesterday, scurry to get where they're going - someplace inside. Someplace warm. In their midst, one man stands out. He has no coat. Instead, he's wrapped himself loosely in a blanket. The cold wind is tearing at it. The frayed ends flap wildly like untethered sails in a storm, like tattered banners left behind on some forgotten battlefield.

The man clutches at his flimsy covering as he hurries on. Like all of us, he's going somewhere this morning. Across from the gleaming skyscraper that awaits me is an old church; a church that offers a modest breakfast for the homeless. Breakfast and a warm place for those who have no place.

I sit in my car at the traffic light as the music plays. The heater is on. I wear a scarf and a North Face jacket. I'm warm enough. I'm comfortable. In a moment or two I'll be drinking hot coffee in a welcoming Starbucks. The enigmatic green Starbucks logo lady with her odd crown will not turn me away. I have the $2.25 price of admission to the world of ordinary, normal people and warm, friendly places.

My battle is not yet over. I have not won, but neither have I been beaten, haven't surrendered. My standard has not touched the ground, my colors are faded but untaken. I march onward into this day. But part of my heart remains behind with a nameless, faceless, blanket-clad man, in the cold. In the dark. In the Med Center.

I wonder about his battles. What malevolent forces real or imagined were arrayed against him? Did he fall for want of courage or strategy or resources or the strong arm of a steadfast ally? Do his losses haunt him? What wounds lie concealed beneath that sad blanket, and what balm might heal this stumbling, suffering soul?

Perhaps I imagine too freely, construct elaborate tales from a flickering, half-formed image embellished by too little sleep. But whatever the truth may be about the man in the blanket, I offer up a simple prayer that he might know that regardless of circumstance, he is still a child of God, no less than any other man.

And he does not walk alone.

Tom Kiske

A Different Universe, A Different God

The multiverse. Everything - all matter, all energy - comprised of infinitesimal vibrating strings. A nearly infinite number of universes and an equally vast number of dimensions. New universes constantly being born. Such is the state of theoretical physics today.

It's more than the human mind can grasp, despite what mathematics commands. Can we "believe" it? Is it more obscure than the idea of a "triune" God, which billions of believers claim to accept? Does, perhaps, this strange new physics render the Holy Trinity *more* believable? Does Heaven lie not above the clouds, but in some alternate universe, some unseen dimension?

What are the religious implications of a physics seemingly more magical than scientific; theories we are called upon to believe absent any observable evidence - indeed, absent even the possibility of observation?

Wiser minds than mine may debate and puzzle out the new interconnects between the secular and non-secular worlds. For me, though, one implication is clear: our old beliefs have drawn our God far too narrowly. Our testamentary concept of a Divinity is too small by several orders of magnitude to encompass the expanded - and expanding - cosmos.

Only the mystics seem to have intuitively grasped this, and long before the emergence of string theory. Only they have dispensed with the bearded, grandfather-god who lays down Commandments and smites the enemies of "His people." Instead, through the ages the mystics have sought to commune with a Spirit at once greater and less definable than the primitive portrait painted by Scripture. They have attempted to know God without the intercession of words and reason, but rather through some older, more diffuse form of intelligence. The same intelligence, perhaps, that may someday afford us the sole means of comprehending the cosmology sketched by 21st Century physics.

An intelligence, it may be, instilled deep within us by the Author of all knowledge and all mystery.

When the Librarian's Away

This story resulted from a writing contest. The challenge was – a group of friends who've been locked in the library overnight find they can enter into any of the books.
(I did not win the contest, but I think it's an OK story).

The library has a starkly different feel at night when the patrons and staff have gone. Always been a friendly and welcoming place during normal hours, now a darker or stranger side seemed to have emerged, at least in my mind. Part of that, of course, might be because Danny, Elaine and I had gotten ourselves locked in.

"Is it just me or is it kinda creepy in here?" Danny asked.

"It is," Elaine said nervously, "but what worries me is whether we'll be going to jail when they find us here tomorrow morning."

"Oh, come on," I chided, "Heck, it's their fault for not checking the study rooms at closing time, not to mention their 'no cell phones' policy."

Elaine went behind the checkout counter and picked up the phone for the land line. "No dial tone," she announced, "They must shut off the phones when they leave."

"Now that's weird," Danny said."

"Well, look, guys," I said, "We're stuck here. Might as well make the best of it."

"Right. How, Tony?" Elaine asked.

"I know – a pajama party!" Danny said, winking at Elaine.

"Dreamer," she said, wandering off, "Let's at least do some exploring."

Danny and I looked at each other, shrugged and headed our separate ways.

I was halfway down one of the aisles of shelves when I first heard the murmuring. It was indistinct, barely audible at all. I stopped, tried to listen more closely. Voices? I couldn't make out words but it sounded like speech. Where the heck is that coming from, I wondered.

While I stood there straining to hear, the books began vibrating. Not the shelves, just the books. Quivering, shaking. *All* the books!

What the heck? This was no earthquake, but what *was* it?

While I watched, fascinated and a bit worried, one slim book looked as though it were trying to work itself loose, wiggle itself off the shelf. I took a step till I stood right in front of the energetic volume. I peeked over the binding to see if maybe Danny was pranking me, jiggling the books, pushing this one out. Nope, nobody there.

As the murmuring grew louder, the book tumbled off the shelf into my hands. It seemed as if it had presented itself to me, demanded my attention. It was Dickens. I opened the cover, flipped to a random page and found myself pulled into the main office of Scrooge & Marley. I don't mean metaphorically pulled into. I don't mean the story captured my attention. No, I was *there*, physically there in that dingy, poorly lit 19th Century office. Ebenezer was sitting at his big desk, scowling over some document while Bob Cratchit labored away at his much smaller desk, scribbling entries into a huge ledger.

Scrooge seemed oblivious to my presence, but Cratchit, well, that was a different matter. He looked directly at me.

"Good evening," he said, "Took you long enough, didn't it?"

I was stunned. "You aren't surprised to see me?"

"Not exactly *you*, mind you, but folks do wander in from time to time," Cratchit said, "and from your peculiar dress, you appear to be from the future –

The Time Machine, perhaps?"

Still reeling, I said, "You get visitors from other, uh, stories?"

"You mean other books?" Cratchit huffed, "Did you think we just sit around on these shelves gathering dust?"

"No offense, sir," I replied, "I just – I didn't know."

"Typical," he snarled, "Didn't know, didn't care. Now I'm thinking you must be from one of those so-called 'modern' works, a romance, maybe a mystery?"

"Well, no," I said, "You see, I'm a real person."

"Oh, yes, I most definitely do see," Cratchit scoffed, "You think everyone from an older generation is somehow less important, less real than you youngsters."

"Not what I meant at all, it's . . . uh, well, how can I put it? I'm not a character in a book."

"Character? Character?" he demanded, his voice growing louder and more strident," What do you mean, *character*?"

As I struggled to find words to calm Cratchit and better explain myself, the door burst open with a crash. Framed in the opening and backlit by London's gas streetlights was the most gigantic person I'd ever seen. "Aaaarrhhh," he roared.

The creature scared the bejeebers out of me, but the little clerk seemed oddly undisturbed. "Just close the door, come in and knock off the sound effects, Frank," he said, "and please, *please* stop banging the door open like that. How many times do I have to tell you?"

"Sorry, Bob," the giant mumbled as he staggered in.

When I had recovered somewhat, I turned to Cratchit, "Who or what is Frank?"

"A thousand pardons," he replied, "allow me to introduce you. Technically, he's The Monster or Frankenstein's Monster, but I try not to be judgmental, so to me he's just plain Frank. By the way, you never told me your name."

"Oh, Tony" I said.

"Well then, Frank, meet O'Tony; O'Tony, Frank."

"Hey, Frank," I said, choosing not to correct Cratchit lest we go round and round again.

"Hey back," Frank grunted diffidently.

"Frank, O'Tony was just explaining that you and I aren't real people but he is," Cratchit said.

I'd had enough. "Oh, for gosh sakes, I'm outta here," I said, heading for the door. A quick glance showed Scrooge remained oblivious to the bizarre goings-on.

"Hold up," Cratchit cried, "We're coming with you!"

"WHAT??"

I quickly scooted thru the door, but when I tried to close it behind me, the two of them easily pushed it open and clambered outside. There the three of us stood in a London street scene that was beginning to waver and fade. In a moment I was back in the library – and so were they! How would I ever explain this to Danny and Elaine?

No point in putting off the inevitable. I headed to the lobby, trailed by Bob Cratchit and the Frankenstein monster.

Then things got really strange. The lobby was a bit crowded. Danny was there with a scruffy looking kid and the two of them were carrying on a conversation with a rather large sorrel horse.

"Uh, Danny?"

"Oh, hi, Tony," he said, "Man, the strangest thing happened."

"Really," I said, "Never would've guessed."

Danny chuckled. "Yeah, looks like you've had some adventures, too. Who are your new friends?"

I told him 'friends' might not be the term I'd use, but introduced my two . . . travel companions. Danny introduced me to Huck Finn. "The horse's name is kinda unpronounceable. I call him Trigger."

"Obvious where you found Huck, but the horse?"

Trigger cleared his throat. "Ahem," he began in an exceptionally well-modulated and cultured baritone, "No mere horse, I am a Houyhnhnm."

"He's sensitive about that," Danny whispered, "Found him in Gulliver's Travels."

"Of course you did," I said, "and how nice you brought him and Huck back with you."

"Not like I had a choice," Danny bristled, "Besides, look what tagged along with you."

"Just a ding-dong minute," Cratchit blustered, "I'm getting pretty tired of being insulted. Like your buddy O'Tony, now you think you're 'real' and better than us?"

"Uh, uh, what he said," Frank added, clearly struggling to form the words.

"What I'm attempting to determine," Trigger said, "is what subspecies of Yahoo are all of you?"

As you can imagine, everyone took offense at that, even though it was coming from a horse . . . er, Houyhnhnm. Huck took off his ragged old hat and threw it at Trigger, where it landed atop his magnificent head, completing the outlandish tableau.

Or maybe not. Elaine suddenly appeared, interrupting the altercation before it boiled over. "What the heck's going on here?" she demanded.

"You wanna take this, Danny?" I asked.

"Ooohhh, no," he replied, "All yours."

"Well, you see Elaine," I began, "we got into these books and . . . uh, when I say 'got into' what I mean is . . ."

"Oh, I know," Elaine chuckled, "Come on in, Atticus."

Stepping from the aisle Elaine had partially blocked was the world's most famous lawyer, bearing a striking resemblance to Gregory Peck. "Gentlemen," he said, tipping his hat, "and Mr. Horse."

"Houyhnhnm," insisted Trigger.

"Bless you," Cratchit chimed in, thinking Trigger had sneezed.

Just when I thought things couldn't get any crazier, a flock of flying monkeys flew in from somewhere, followed by - who else? The Wicked Witch of the West, cackling and snarling.

"Oh, Elaine," I groaned, "you didn't!"

"I did. I followed the yellow brick road. Sorry."

"Sip, anyone?" asked Huck, producing a flask from his back pocket.

By that point we were all ready for a drink or two. Huck generously passed around the flask. Trigger had a little trouble, but Frank stepped up and held the flask to the Houyhnhnm's lips. "Not bad for Yahoo booze," Trigger said, "Thanks, Frank."

After a couple of belts everyone got much friendlier. Even the witch loosened up. Heck, she even told a few jokes. A bit lame, but we all chuckled anyway and stopped calling her the wicked witch. At length the hour grew late and we were all getting drowsy. I think we must've even dozed for a while. I know I did.

Until - from somewhere deep in the farthest aisle a powerful voice called out, "Hark! What light through yonder window breaks?"

It was dawn and as the morning sun began streaming through the library's many windows, our motley literary crew grew dim, at length fading away entirely. Now it was just Danny, Elaine and me.

"How are we going to explain this," Danny said, "Nobody will believe any of it."

"They'll think we're nuts – or on drugs," Elaine added.

"We're not saying anything. Nothing at all about . . . uh, them."

"Yeah, but then how'll we explain that," Danny said, pointing to a conspicuous lump right in the middle of the floor, "the horse left a pungent souvenir behind."

"Houyhnhnm," I automatically corrected.

Elaine grinned. "Bless you," she said with a wink.

From somewhere far off came a tiny, child's voice, "and God bless us, every one."

Cloud Watcher

How long has it been since you watched clouds? Not seen clouds or noticed clouds or been peripherally aware of clouds as you went about your business, but just sat and watched and did nothing else?

I arise earlier than I wanted this morning. The house is quiet. I have my cereal. Read a newspaper, and, it being Sunday, brew some "real" coffee – not the instant stuff of a weekday. I pour myself a cup, tuck the second newspaper under my arm and retreat to the back porch to enjoy the mild 79-degree break in the hot summer weather.

A mockingbird who's taken up residence nearby begins his enthusiastic warbling – surely the inspiration for the pop number, "*I got a song ain't got no melody.*" More accurately, I suppose, it's not that the mockingbird's song has no melody, but rather that it has an infinite number of them. I put the newspaper aside, listen a while. Water from the small porch fountain gurgles. Tree leaves rustle in the gentle breeze.

From the woods, swifts dart out and put on their aerial show in pursuit of what I know not. Their breakfast, perhaps, or a mate. Dragonflies flit and hover as well. A neighbor's cat punctuates the morning with an occasional soft meow. Wants in, maybe. Wants something.

Across the way, a pickup truck traverses the bridge. He's lost. That road goes nowhere. A moment later, the truck reappears headed back the other way. Many searches are underway this morning.

The birds direct my eye upward. There was rain last night; the sky is clear and blue. Only a few small, wispy cumulus drift overhead, moving slowly northward. My attention is caught by them, my newspaper forgotten. I no longer wish to read. I want to watch.

It's a slow-motion parade. There's no cadence, no regimentation. Clouds abjure organization. Their northerly drift aside, they appear randomly. Some are so ephemeral they evaporate before my eyes. Others, although gauzy, have more to them; hold together as they move into the distance.

Clouds are gathering now and changing from white to gray. More clouds now than sky. The smell of coming rain is in the air. I am not looking for shapes in these clouds. I am not doing anything. I am passive, a mere observer. Soon, despite the coffee my mind goes fuzzy as the clouds. I slump down further into the chair, rest my head against the back pillow. It's not drowsiness that pours over me, but a cloud-calm I've not known for a long while. A long, long while.

Perhaps because my gaze is upward, or maybe because of the peacefulness I've settled into, my easy mind turns to Him. I pose my usual questions. Wait.

And wait.

Restfulness does not come naturally to me, nor does it long abide. I still watch, but now I am also one of the seekers. But no answer comes. No voice is heard.

It's OK. I look around once more. Maybe this – all this – is the answer, the only answer.

It's enough.

The Least of These

"Inasmuch as ye have done it unto one of the least of these my brethren, ye have done it unto me."
Mathew 25:40

October 31:

The storm blew in from the north at dusk, just as tiny goblins would otherwise have been setting out in search of treats. It was a cold and blustery wind, the pounding rain punctuated by thunder and lightning. Wise parents would not permit their costumed charges to wander wet streets amid such a deluge. Given a choice, even adults would not leave the warmth of home in the face of nature's chill reminder of the season.

Some, though, are not afforded the luxury of choice. Among these unfortunates, an older black couple we noticed as they trudged along the road. The man struggled to push a shopping cart laden with what was likely the sum of their worldly possessions. The storm had been forecast to be brutal, and the troubled sky and rising gusts warned the worst what yet to come, and soon. As the homeless couple sought a measure of shelter beneath a Starbucks canopy the same unspoken thought occurred to my wife and I: where will they spend this wretched night? Then the immediate corollary: can we help?

But we were driving and before thoughts transformed to action, we were half a mile beyond the sorrowful scene, turning into our neighborhood, distracted by other matters and the routine of arriving home. And so, Halloween came and went, only a handful of determined children braving lulls in the downpour to ring our doorbell and relieve us of the merest fraction of the stockpiled sweets we'd planned to award a herd of masked marauders that never materialized.

It was later, in sleepless midnight hours that what we'd passed by so hurriedly returned in haunting images and imaginings. Why didn't we react more rapidly and compassionately to those fellow humans in need? Who were those two, and what fell circumstances led them to be afoot and vulnerable and so terribly alone against the gathering darkness? What might we have found if we'd stopped to help - were they brought low by their own failings and misdeeds? Were they mentally unbalanced, as likely to scream at us as welcome our assistance?

Or were they Mary and Joseph, appearing along our path to offer a reminder that salvation is earned not by worshipful words or pious professions of belief, but through the love we show fellow travelers we encounter along the road of life?

Who You Are, Who You Were

The way you think of yourself changes over time. This is no stunning revelation. Still, a line from a movie brought it home. A young woman says something about a person "walking into my life."

When you're young, life seems to stretch endlessly before you. More, it is an amorphous thing, its contours fluid, its definition vague, its colors transitory. There's ample room for wonder. For surprise. For someone to walk into your life and by his or her presence fundamentally change everything. And change is welcome. We are malleable. We bend with the bender. Always it is morning.

Too gradually to notice, we lose that. As our epiphyses solidify, as our veins calcify, so our very life often grows into a hard, inflexible thing. Our dimensions are measured and recorded in our own permanent ledger. *This* is me. *That* is not me.

It is, I suppose, a natural progression, but that does not alter the fact it is also a closing-in. A sealing off of one's perimeter. It is a fence we erect around ourselves, within which we voluntarily confine ourselves. Our selves.

Then we scurry around, busy ourselves maintaining our personal fortress against the unknown – an unknown which has come to represent a threat rather than the source of surprise and magic it once was.

But then one morning you're on your way to work, focused on the tasks that lie before you. You stop for gas. Standing beside your car as the tank fills you glance upward. The sky is bright blue. Cotton clouds drift slowly, peacefully across the great expanse. Deep within, some vestige of who you once were whispers gently, "Oh . . ."

ALTERNATE ENDINGS

In the Slipstream of Time

Wow
Holy sh*t
Lookit dem clouds
Dude!
What's for lunch?
Whatever
Groovy
Have a nice day
Far Out

May 10, 2014

My mother's birthday. She'd be 99. Eleven years she's been gone and it feels a different world in her absence. It is still difficult to look at her picture. To do so drains my heart. For a moment I am crippled by the memory of her.

Does time heal?

To some degree, I suppose. The hurt may be a thin slice less, the scar tissue grown tough and less easily ripped open; faster, perhaps, to knit. There *is* a healing, then, comes with time. But never a cure. The wound remains. We know it's there. We seek to protect it. Guarding, as we would a torn muscle.

My mother has four great-grandchildren now, two she never met during her lifetime. Does she know of them now, I wonder. Does the Spirit of her rejoice in the freshness and growth of her great-grandchildren's beautiful souls? Does she watch over them in whatever manner is given her to do so?

Do my mother and father abide happily together in a place of peace and love, surrounded by their parents, brothers and sisters? Have all their wounds been taken away, along with every care and worry and woe?

Do they see thru the fog of time more clearly than our poor senses allow? Do they know in the depth of their being what some among us may glimpse for but a fleeting moment - that yesterday, today and tomorrow are one? If given them to do so, would they speak to me, telling me and that every infinitesimal particle of them is joined to me, as I am joined to them, to you, to everyone and to all there ever was or ever will be? Would they reiterate the Galilean's wisdom: that what holds together all of space and time and life is love.

My birthday wish, May 10, 2014. Blow out the candles.

𝓝o 𝓟lace for 𝓢anta

I'm in Starbucks this morning. These young people are so *serious* about their coffee. A 30-something ahead of me in line (yes, *in line* for coffee) has a complicated order, ending with a "double-shot" of something or other. Moments later, still somber-faced, he reminds the clerk* he's forgotten his "punkin bread." By now I'm grinning to myself.

Is it me who's out of step? Probably. That's my modus vivendi - out of step.

Which brings me to the ho's. Here's the issue that's been troubling me of late: why does Santa always - *always* - laugh with a "ho-ho-ho?" Why do you never hear "ho-ho" or "ho-ho-ho-ho?" Is there something significant, perhaps magical, about three ho's? Only thing I can think is, does it perhaps relate way back to the first Christmas? Has the story become distorted over the intervening millennia? Is it possible He was visited in the manger not by the three kings of legend, but rather by three common ho's? Is that the origin of the mandatory ho-ho-ho?

It might explain those gifts of perfume. You know, the frankincense and myrrh. Odd gifts for kings to be bearing, but perfectly logical for ho's. Is Santa saluting the oldest profession?

Heresy, or history? You decide.

Then there's this: who says "ho" when they laugh? Isn't it more like "ha?" Are we to assume Santa has a cold or sinus infection that drops his laugh down an octave or two? If so, wouldn't it be more like "ho-ho-cough-cough?" Instead of cookies and milk, should we be leaving the poor guy a couple of Benadryl?

For that matter, what's so funny? What's got Santa so tickled? I never understood this. It's another mystery. Surely the old elf, jolly though he may be, wouldn't be laughing for no reason. Anyone who laughs for no reason (be it with ho's or ha's) would be considered, well, nuts.

Oh, man. Santa, you'd best stay away from Starbucks. Way too serious for the likes of you. You'll be trading in that red suit for one of those white jackets with the extra-long sleeves.

---

*NOTE: I always forget the terminology. Are we supposed to call them baritones? Barleycorns? Sandinistas?

An Ordinary Morning

As mornings go there was little to mark this one different from a hundred before it or a hundred yet to come. I awoke within the broad parameters of my usual time of arising, the bathroom scale confirmed that I'd neither gained nor lost weight. I splashed water on my face, donned the same casual attire I'd taken off the previous night, made my way to the kitchen and prepared my usual little breakfast. My wife & I enjoyed a typical morning conversation about newspaper articles and the TV program we'd watched yesterday evening. I shaved, showered, dressed and set out for work. It was all quite ordinary.

Until.

As I drove slowly up the street, only a few doors from home I spied D---- rolling her trash can down the driveway to the curb for pickup. I waved and received a half-smile in return. An unmistakably sad half-smile. How long has her husband been gone? How long since he was shot and killed in the performance of his duties? Is it four years? Five?

Despite my inability to compute elapsed time, the memory of that morning remains starkly clear: my son calling me at work with the terrible news - news so shocking that at first the mind can neither encompass nor accept it. The memory of the days that followed is no less indelibly etched in the mind and soul - the outpouring of heartfelt grief from a community robbed of a good man, a good life cut short.

And if those memories still haunt my heart, how much more so must they torment D----? The smile that she never quite formed - was she thinking it was on a morning like this, a morning with little to mark it different from a hundred before it, an ordinary morning - it was a morning like this that the world ended.

Shitty things happen in life. Horrible, unfathomable, unfair things. Things that shouldn't happen but do. Things that take a toll, exact a price, leave a cruel and lingering scar. Things beyond our power to understand, prevent or mend. How are we to deal with such a somber, undeniable truth?

Philosophers and prophets have struggled with this question through the ages. I am neither, but I wonder if the lesson in trouble and tragedy might be as simple as this: that there is something precious in the ordinary, that an undistinguished morning is a treasure, and that tomorrow is a gift we may not be given.

And from such knowledge perhaps we might redouble our commitment to fashioning a better world with the tools available to us within the scope of our reach and our ability. Nowhere is the wish better expressed than in the Prayer of Saint Francis:

"Lord, make me an instrument of your peace:
Where there is hatred, let me sow love;
Where there is injury, pardon;
Where there is doubt, faith;
Where there is despair, hope;
Where there is darkness, light;
Where there is sadness, joy."

These words and their continuation may or may not have been written by Francis of Assisi over 800 years ago, but they resonate today. They resonate this very moment. The precious ordinary moment in which we live.

How Grinchmeister Downsized Christmas

He'd been around so long nobody could remember a time when he *wasn't* around. His hair and flowing beard, it seemed, had *always* been white, just as he'd always been a bit overweight and had always spread cheer with his robust, jovial laughter. He's been with the company since its inception and many thought him largely responsible for its success and the universal esteem in which it was held through-out its global venue. Now, though, things were changing.

First there'd been the corporate buy-out, a hostile takeover, really. Now the new management team was on board and they had their own idea about how the operation should be run. Lean And Mean were the watchwords now, with emphasis on the latter. Staff cuts became routine. Still, it shocked everyone the day the finally called *him* on the carpet.

Donald J. Grinchmeister, the new CEO, sat scowling behind his expensive new oak desk the size of a small boat as his secretary showed the old fellow in. "You sent for me, sir?" he said.

"Yes, yes, Kris," Grinchmeister croaked, forcing a smile that was more akin to a grimace. "Sit down, please, we have some important matters to go over."

Kris slowly eased his ample bulk into one of the leather side chairs, noting that the front legs had been deliberately cut shorter than the back ones, an old trick designed to make the occupant uncomfortable.

"Kris, I'll get right to the point," Grinchmeister said, focusing sternly on the old man. "Polar Industries Inc. has certain expectations for this enterprise, and frankly, you haven't been measuring up."

"Well, this is a busy season for us," Kris began, "once we get through this, maybe we can ..."

"No. We need action now," Grinchmeister interrupted, "We've got to re-do this operation from top to bottom. Get on a more profitable footing right away."

"We've always managed to make ends meet, Mr. G.," Chris objected, "but what changes do you think are needed?"

"First off, all those elves have to go!"

"What? You can't mean that." Kris stammered, "Why, we've always employed elves here. They're excellent, skilled workers. Some of their families go back almost as far as the Missus and me."

"Yes, yes, I'm sure that's true," Grinchmeister huffed impatiently, "but think of the labor costs. The elf wage scale is simply uneconomical. You should never have let them hook up with those Snow-White dwarves and unionize the factory. That damn shop steward, Grumpy, is nothing but trouble with his demands and grievances."

"I've always got along with him okay," Kris said, "besides, what can we do? We're under contract, you know."

"Bullshit!" Grinchmeister yelled, "What we're gonna do is offshore our manufacturing."

"Off shore? But we've always worked here at the North Pole."

"And that's part of the problem: stale thinking. Listen, Kris, it's a global economy, now. We can get our product made in China for under half what we're paying those elves – and no union problems!"

"But...but..."

"No 'buts' about it." Grinchmeister barked, "You better get with the program or we'll replace *you*."

"Now wait just a doggone minute," Kris protested.

"No, you wait." Grinchmeister interrupted, slamming his fist on the desk, "Some of the folks at the home office have thought all along that you're part of the problem."

"What? How?"

"You're out of touch, Kris. Maybe you're just too old for this business anymore. I mean look at you – that goofy red suit with the white fur trim, that silly hat and boots – who dresses like that these days? And let's face it – you could lose a few pounds."

"But kids expect me to look like this," Kris cried.

"Wrong again." scoffed Grinchmeister, "Today's kids wear jeans and t-shirts. They're into Transformers, video games like Minecraft, cell phone apps. Hell, they'd just laugh at you. You need a new look, a new image."

"Image? What image? This is just me, what I've always been. It's ... it's *traditional.*"

"But that's not enough anymore. In fact, we've hired a branding consultant to repackage the whole program." Grinchmeister said, striding over to the side door, "Get a load of *this!*"

The door flew open and in hopped a Schwartzenegger clone in a skin-tight silver jumpsuit. Over one massive shoulder he carried a huge gold lame' sack laced up with a twisted silver cord. "Ho-ho freakin' ho," he growled in menacing Dirty Harry fashion.

"No, no, this can't be right," Kris muttered.

"Hey, wait 'til you get a gander of the updated Mrs. Claus," laughed Grinchmeister.

In through the door rolled an AI-powered robot, featuring a somewhat feminine "face" along with prominent silicone boobs and buttocks. "What do *you* want for Xmas, little boy?" the robot purred seductively, "Just tell Alexa."

Kris's mind reeled. What the devil were these fools up to? They were going to destroy traditions going back hundreds of years. "You can't do this," he screamed at Grinchmeister, "I won't permit it!"

"Ha! What exactly do you think you can do about it?"

"Why, I ... I won't let you use my reindeer and sleigh."

"Who needs 'em?" Grinchmeister laughed, "We're shipping everything FedEx this year, maybe even working with Amazon on drone delivery. That'll work great with our new standardized gift packs."

"Standardized ... what's that?" Kris mumbled, now thoroughly dazed by what was unfolding around him.

Grinchmeister explained that Polar Industries had partnered with several sponsors that were underwriting the cost of sample gift packs containing products they were anxious to have distributed to the world's kids.

"Well, what will the little ones be getting," Kris asked anxiously.

"You'll love this." Grinchmeister grinned, "Thanks to the generosity of the Tobacco Institute, Big Pharma and the NRA, every boy and girl all over the world will wake up Christmas morning with a carton of Camels, a vaping pen, a box of 9mm slugs and a blister pack of Oxy."

"Oh, no," Kris wailed, collapsing to the floor, "Oh, no, no, no. no. no!"

Some say Kris's mind just snapped that day and he was never the same again. Polar Industries forced him into immediate retirement, then whisked him off to a sanitarium where, under the stringent new Medicare rules, he received exactly two days of therapy before being tossed out into the snow.

Fortunately, an elf search party located him and returned him to the little cottage at the North Pole, where he and Mrs. Kringle lived a reclusive but reasonably comfortable life for three years on Kris's modest pension, until Grinchmeister raided the plan and absconded with the funds to the Caribbean, where he lived happily ever after.

Meanwhile, the Kringles were forced to sell their home and are currently eking out a marginal existence cleaning windshields and from occasional guest appearances on TV talk shows.

In some ways it's kind of a sad tale, but, shoot, that's progress!

𝓟arable 𝓘mprobable

Sunday. A good day for an epiphany, right? I mean, sorta the *right* day. Made me wonder about what happened later.

I awoke stiff and achy. There was work to be done, work that did not go well with stiff and achy; domestic house cleaning that required bending, kneeling, lifting. Challenging for a go whose body no longer bends willingly or well.

Nevertheless, in time the work got done and surprisingly, I felt better afterwards, decided to push my luck and take a short walk. As I made my way down the driveway, my eyes were drawn upward. Interesting things were taking place on that vast palette. A bright blue background was being overlayed with swirls in multiple hues of gray. It was so beautiful and stirring that spontaneously and uncharacteristically I was moved to thank God. I thanked him doubly: once for His unparalleled artistry and again for imbuing me with the faculty for appreciating such grand works.

I'd not gone far when a light breeze set the leaves rustling and caressed my face with the first cool hint of pending Autumn. Once again I was compelled to offer up my gratitude for this spirit-lifting experience. As I walked on, I passed a house with Sunday's newspaper lying on the sidewalk. I stepped over it, but for some reason I was drawn back to glance down at the front-page headline:

Elderly Man Beaten to Death

With that, my sense of the morning was chilled; a shift so abrupt and unexpected that a more emotional fellow might have stumbled. Instead, a question formed unbidden in my mind: is there some meaning, some lesson I'm supposed to take from this jarring juxtaposition of enchantment and dismay? Did God program this unsettling sequence? If so, what Divine wisdom am I to draw from it – never get *too* happy? Beauty and joy are short-lived on this plane ere His Kingdom come?

Or has the God of love some evil counterpart whose ire I invoked with my lavish expressions of gratitude to his arch-enemy? Did some spiteful demon toss that newspaper in my path while snickering, "See? He ain't so great. Take a gander at *this* shit!"

Or was there just a sky, a breeze and a newspaper there on Barrington Pointe Drive that Sunday morning? Only that and a man prone to search for larger meanings, and to wonder ....

𝒲𝒶𝓇𝑒𝒽𝑜𝓊𝓈𝑒𝓈 𝒥 𝐻𝒶𝓋𝑒 𝒦𝓃𝑜𝓌𝓃

As I reflect on my working career, it strikes me I've spent a heckuva lot of time in various warehouses: Clorox, Rawlings Sporting Goods – two different times – two laundries and Smith Corona. But it was at International Shoe Company in the late 60's I got my informal, on-the-job Master's in Business and learned how things can get way out of hand in a warehouse.

The company had launched a major project, investing millions of dollars in an effort they believed would save money once fully implemented. At that time, "coding" was done in binary machine language (0's and 1's) and the only way to interact with a computer was via punch cards. The job of keypunch operator was a skilled one that commanded a good salary. International had an entire keypunch department, employing dozens of operators typing away, clackety-clack on their keypunch machines to enter orders from retail shoe stores across America. It worked well, but it was a big expense for the company.

Then, a new development in technology seemed to offer International a far less costly way to enter orders: optical scanning. No more high-paid keypunch operators. Instead, unskilled (i.e., low-paid) clerks would mark up paper documents the size of punch cards. They'd be fed into an IBM 1418 optical scanner. Bye-bye keypunch operators.

Brilliant! What could possibly go wrong? As it turned out, lots of things.

First, you can't just hand clerks a bunch of scan forms and say, here, start filling these out. It took several different forms to enter an order, and completing them out meant using a special pen to make little marks that represented letters and numbers. If you're a certain age, you may recall doing something similar for high school or college exams, but it was brand new to our order-entry clerks and it was much harder. As head of the Systems Department, I was responsible, together with my group, a bunch of guys about my age, for designing the forms, preparing a guidebook and holding a series of training sessions. This seriously detracted from our habit of sneaking off to play whiffle ball on our mostly-empty warehouse floor.

Entering an order was an exceptionally complicated task which could require as many as ten different scan forms. Completing just one form wasn't easy. It demanded good fine motor skills to make those marks, each had to be a perfectly straight line of about 3/8" between two tiny x's. A number could be entered with one mark, but a letter took two. Here are the "Five Rules of Scanning" from Exhibit C in our training manual:

Only scan marks may appear in the scan field
The scan sheets must be kept clean and flat
Make only one stroke per mark
Marks must go all the way from x to x but beyond
Keep the sheets in the proper sequence

A separate exhibit listed the proper sequence of forms, the form names and numbers, whether the document was mandatory or optional and how many of each document could be used for an order. Without our manual as a reference, the clerks – many of whom had only an elementary school education - would've been lost little sheep. Even with it, many struggled with the details or just couldn't master the art of making those little marks. A mis-marked form, one that wasn't "clean and flat" or one that stuck out a bit from the stack fed into the scanner resulted in a huge, jumbled mess of a paper jam. Then all the forms had to be re-marked from scratch.

Additionally, the forms themselves had to meet exacting tolerances or they wouldn't feed properly through the optical scanner. Our initial supplier was IBM, but a whole batch of their forms were slightly off, causing – guess what – huge, jumbled mess of a paper jam and hours of wasted time. It fell to me to solve the problem, which meant investigating and finally changing suppliers. Once Moore Business Forms took over, that problem was mostly behind us. Others weren't.

As part of International's project, they built a huge new warehouse near Jefferson City, Missouri. Unlike warehouses in the past, this one was all on one story. No more time wasted riding an elevator between floors. Plus, the new warehouse was to be automated! The entire warehouse was designed to minimize time and maximize efficiency, meaning cut the cost of filling orders. The basic idea was once orders were scanned, the computer would break them down into "a day's pick" which was sent to the warehouse. Instead of running all over the place grabbing the different models, styles and sizes Joe's Shoe Store had ordered, pickers would just pull as many Poll Parrot Debby-style ordered by all the shoe stores. He'd affix a computer-generated label to each shoe box identifying the customer that ordered it.

Once picked, shoes were loaded one by one onto a conveyor belt that lifted them 25 or 30 feet into the air. Gravity did the rest via roller conveyors. One such conveyor ran almost the whole length of the warehouse, past row upon row of side roller conveyors at a right angle to the main one. Each side line represented one customer. As a shoe box entered the main conveyor, a man read the coded label the picker had affixed to it, then entered the numbers on a keyboard. When a shoe box reached the conveyor for, say, Joe's Shoe Store, a little pneumatic hammer would pop out and knock the box off the main conveyor into the side conveyor for Joe's. Eventually, this conveyor would fill up with all the shoe's Joe's had ordered.

It was a thing of beauty to bring a tear to the eye of an efficiency expert or a bottom-line oriented CEO. But it had one flaw.

My Systems Department needed to grasp the whole operation of the new system so we could explain it to the scan clerks we were charged with training. At least that was the argument we used to justify an educational field trip to Jeff City and, you know, away from the office. We couldn't all go, so I chose Bob M. to accompany me for no reason other than I liked him and he was a fun guy. At the last minute, we were told an older fellow from another department would accompany us, possibly as a chaperone for us wild and crazy youngsters.

The old guy's name was Milt. He'd been at International forever. We knew him. Everybody knew him. He was OK and we didn't mind having him along, but he was a little *different*. To get a feel for this fellow, think about the Milt character in the movie <u>Office Space</u>. The guy with the coke bottle glasses and the red, swingline stapler. Unlike the movie, I think the company was actually paying our Milt, although I can't be sure.

Anyway, once the three of us got to Jeff City and walked into the big, new facility, we were greeted by the warehouse manager, who insisted we don hard hats before he led us on a tour of the operation. We weren't far into the tour before the reason for the protective headgear and the flaw in the system became hilariously clear.

We were walking around looking up at the massive system of conveyor belts when the manager suddenly shouted, "STOP! Don't go under there!"

We did stop, and as we looked down the main conveyor line, we beheld something out of Alice in Wonderland or maybe Gulliver's Travels: shoe box lids drifting down from above. Not one or two of them. Not a dozen of them. Score upon score of shoe box lids rained down and kept raining down. It was a cardboard downpour! Little lids from toddler's shoes, larger lids from ladies' shoes, Big ol' lids from men's shoes and boots; black lids, red lids, lids of all colors, some plain, others with fancy designs. The warehouse floor was six inches deep in shoe box lids!

Clearly embarrassed, the warehouse manager explained with an exacerbated sigh. "Those pneumatic hammers hit the boxes too hard." he said, "Knocks the lids off."

We asked if the hammers couldn't be adjusted. "Working on it," he said, "but when we reduce their power, they don't punch the boxes off into the side sorting lanes. They just stay on the main line all the way to the end where they all pile up and start spilling over. Then instead of just lids, we get lids, boxes and shoes tumbling down."

"What a mess," I said.

"Yeah. I got a crew of a dozen guys doin' nothin' but picking up box lids!"

So much for efficiency. So much for cost savings. But surely worthy of a Wharton case study or an MBA thesis.

Later, Bob, Milt and I decided to mull the situation over at a local bar, discovering a potential tourist draw the Jefferson City Chamber of Commerce had somehow overlooked or chose not to exploit: cheap beer. Also, entertainment. The bar's décor featured the usual assortment of colorful signs advertising an assortment of beer brands, predominantly Budweiser. Hamm's (from the land of sky-blue waters) took it up a level, though.

On their prominently displayed sign, an idealized bucolic scene unfolded in motion under the Hamm's logo. Meadows, trees, underbrush, streams and a small pond painted on an endless translucent back-lit belt went round and round, round and round. If you squinted, it was a little like what you might see if you were riding on a train watching the scenery through the window as you passed. Except, of course, that the scene repeated every 60 seconds or so. Milt was fascinated.

After several rounds of drinks, Bob and I ran out of Jeff City warehouse jokes and grew a bit restless. We paid the tab and got up to leave in hopes of finding a livelier joint somewhere. Milt rose too, but not without some disappointment and a mild protest.

"Aww," he complained, eyes still on the Hamm's sign, "I wanted to see the end of the movie."

A Puppy's Perspective

Worry. It's a big part of most people's lives. There are just so many things to worry about. Even in a relatively stable and affluent country like the U.S. we worry over the economy, terrorism at home & abroad, war, politics, natural disasters, disease, climate change, pollution, medical care, as well as a host of individual concerns like family, finances, work, appearance, aging, love, sickness and sex, to mention just a few.

By contrast as I'm driving here this morning there's a black dog - a mutt - in the back seat of the car next to me. As puppy passengers will do, his head is poked out of the window. He (or she) is just looking around, maybe enjoying the feel of the breeze on his little doggie face. He does not seem to be experiencing any of the anxieties to which his chauffeur and other nearby drivers are prone. A little anthropomorphizing might impute the little fellow's thoughts, *"Oh boy, where we goin'? Are we there yet? Is there gonna be something good to eat? Can we run and play? I bet this is gonna be great!"*

Who knows - maybe puppy's being hauled off to the vet to have his masculinity whacked off. Could be, but he's not worrying about it now. He's just enjoying the ride and eagerly anticipating fun that may or may not really lie in his immediate future. If he falls asleep and wakes up with less of himself to lick, he'll deal with that then.

We could learn a lot from a mutt with his head sticking out a car window.

The Revolt of the Lesser-Known Gods

One day a group of Greco-Roman gods most people have never heard of got together after work to let off steam. After a few drinks it was clear most of them had serious grievances with the administration.

"*Let's face it, man,*" said Flatulatus, "*we do a lot of heavy lifting around here, but do we get any respect?*" As usual, he punctuated his comment with an audible and nasty-smelling gaseous emission.

"Hades no," moaned Infectus, "I mean my job's pretty darn important. Without me and my diseases them humans might live forever, overpopulating the whole joint."

"Right on, brother," burped Chubbia, "Atlas is already starting to bitch about how heavy it's getting."

"Who put Zeus in charge, anyway?" demanded Flatulatus.

Minerva, who was standing at the far end of the bar, said "Well, don't y'all remember that business with the Titans, and how Zeus ..."

"Zeus, Schmoose!" yelled Interuptia," Who asked you, anyway?"

"*Yeah, @#%&$ you!*" screamed Vulgarus.

"Hear, hear. Woman got her min-nerva" chuckled Punnia.

Yummia finished the cupcake she was munching on, pushed aside the ice cream and cake in front of her, cleared her throat and said, "*So, what do we do? Uh, we need a union or something?*"

"At least a caucus," suggested Politico. "We'd need a catchy name, though."

"Yes. Something tricky," added Prevaricatus, "maybe 'freedom' something."

"Already taken," laughed Minerva as everyone glared at her, *" Y'all are really dumb."*

"Ain't neither," protested Ignoramus, "We know lotsa stuff fer sure an' we don't need no smarty pants, because who axed you – remember? Huh huh!"

"We're not getting anywhere here," complained Avarishus, "We oughta be working on how to make a buck."

Indifferentio, who'd been casually observing the whole thing from a table in the back, got up and headed for the door. *"Good luck,"* he said, *" but this is y'all's problem. See ya later. "*

That really put a damper on the discussion. Then Laziass yawned, pronounced the meeting boring and said if they were looking volunteers to count him out. Then he promptly dozed off. Nobody said anything for several minutes as the mood turned dark and gloomy. Then Bacchus walked in.

"How 'bout a drinkypoo, everyone?" he said with a big grin.

Rainfall

Overnight and into the early morning hours the rain fell gently. There was no storm, no thunder, no lightning, no strong winds. The dark heavy rain clouds lingered overhead for a time, until scattered away by the strengthening sun.

The air and all it touches has been washed clean.

It's early April, the time of returning life. Colors leached away by Winter's cold, emerge anew, fresh and bright. So many shades of green have the power to soothe the eye and the spirit. In familiar woods we love to walk, along hard surfaced roads we've traveled drearily for months, wildflowers burst forth, painting petals across the landscape palette in hues of red and blue, yellow and pink. Their awakening awakens something within us; something that was lulled asleep so slowly under Winter's spell we knew not that it slumbered during that dark and dormant season.

No one needs flowers until they do. No one needs drink until they thirst, and Spring is the thirsty season. We forget the things that are real until the warming time dissipates the gloom, reminding us where we live and why we live.

The hope of mankind is not our restless minds, not our dexterous hands, but a car pulled over to the shoulder, a young family spilling eagerly out and children frolicking through His garden, carefree and joyful, happy hearts abloom, fed by a wise simplicity, sustained by the gentle rain-rhythm of the wild and natural beauty that sings to the miracle souls inside them.

Inside us all.

The Hyfrecator 2000

It was with some trepidation that Tom entered the coldly antiseptic offices of his dermatologist for a return visit related to a small growth the doctor had biopsied a week prior. With their usual unsmiling efficiency, Tom was checked in, then escorted to Examining Room 3 by the buxom young nurse Bubbles.

"Sit there," nurse Bubbles commanded with a smirk, "the doctor will be in soon."

Tom sat, fidgeted, poked around the room and worried until the doctor swished in some 30 minutes later, together with his buxom young nurse. "Bad news, Tom," the doctor grinned, "We're gonna have to use the Hyfrecator 2000 on you."

"No, no," Tom pleaded, "Please, Doctor Mengele, not the Hyfrecator 2000."

"Ha, YESS, the Hyfrecator 2000," Mengele screeched, "You didn't think we'd let you off without a good hyfrecatin' did ya?"

"But . . . but . . ."

"Secure the patient, nurse Bubbles."

"But . .. but . . . I don't WANNA be secured," Tom protested.

"Oh, don't be such a baby," buxom nurse Bubbles sneered, pushing Tom onto the exam table and strapping him securely in place. "Shall I loosen his belt, Doctor," she asked.

"You ALWAYS wanna do that," Doctor Mengele exclaimed, "Sorry to disappoint, but we're gonna work on this bozo's face."

"My . . . my FACE?" the unfortunate Tom cried.

"Yes, that ugly puss of yours gonna get hyfrecated," the doctor yelled."

"Well what do I get to do?" nurse Bubbles whined, stamping her foot.

"Oh, OK, how 'bout you take his wife into Exam 5, hook her up with the old doofus in there?"

"Oooooo," Nurse Bubbles exclaimed, "Fun! I've already loosened his belt."

"Fine, now scram. I gots to get to work here."

As Nurse Bubbles attempted to shove her into the Exam room with the old doofus, Tom's wife, shrieked, "Who the heck is THAT?" and fled down the hall and out the front door, dialing 9-1-1 as she ran. Nurse Bubbles shrugged, then entered Exam 5 herself, loosening her tight-fitting nurse outfit with its really, really short skirt.

Back in the other room Doctor Mengele fired up his trusty Hyfrecator 2000, twisting the dial up to Warp 2.

"Pockecta-pocketa-pocketa" went the Hyfrecator.

"Hee-hee-heee" went Doctor Mengele.

"Ow-ow-ow," went Tom.

"Sizzle-sizzle-sizzle" went the skin on Tom's previously handsome face.

Meanwhile, different but equally strange noises came from behind the door to Exam Room 5.

Note:

The preceding tale is based loosely - very, very loosely - on actual events. Unlike the HAL 9000, The Hyfecator 2000 is a real device doctors use to cauterize wounds. "Cauterize" is a word doctors use because it sounds way better than "burn." It does not actually feel - or smell - any better though.

Sciency Stuff

A Socratic Dialog between "LKW," a generic female-type college student and "GpK" an equally generic (but wise) old grandfatherly fellow.

LKW: So, Grandpa, how's about vampires and stuff?

GpK: Well, you know vampires aren't real, right?

LKW: Huh?

GpK: No, that's right. Lots of what you see in movies and books is just made up.

LKW: Woa!

GpK: No werewolves or zombies, either.

LKW: But . . . but . . .

GpK: Nope, they're all merely fignewtons of the imagination.

LKW: So, then is there *anything* scary?

GpK: Sure. Global warming.

LKW: I was thinking more in terms of Creatures of The Darkness.

GpK: Only thing in that category would be - - - BOYS!

LKW: That seems to be a consistent theme with you, but hey, is there anything I can do like if I wanted to actually protect myself against, uh, boys?

GpK: You betcha, but you can forget about crosses and wolfbane and garlic . . . well, maybe garlic but you'd have to eat a whole lot of it. Mostly, tho, try this 3-part approach: First, dress really, really conservatively. I mean, think burka. Secondly, try not to jiggle much when you walk. And finally, never, never EVER smile at a boy.

LKW: Wowee, that sounds like good advice. Lemme write that down. (Sounds of writing and giggling).

GpK: Wait, there's lots more.

LKW: I gotta go now. Bye.

GpK: But . . . but . . .

The Fellowship of 912 Elm

. . . you and I are old;
Old age hath yet his honor and his toil; . . .
Tho' much is taken, much abides; and tho'
We are not now that strength which in old days
Moved earth and heaven, that which we are, we
are;

<u>Ulysses</u>, Alfred, Lord Tennyson

912 Elm Street, Columbia, Missouri, 1963-64. An odd assemblage of boys of diverse background thrown together in a three-story wood frame co-op house, hoping for a college education with maybe a little fun thrown in. Or maybe the other way 'round.

Fifty years later, old men now, eleven of us gather at Watermill Cove in Branson to . . . to what? To see what happens? To renew our friendship? Simply to see one another again?

We're drawn together because of a bond formed over fifty years ago. Many of us haven't seen one another for most of that time. Our paths since 912 have been as varied as they were before - cattle ranchers, pilots, a radio personality, a computer expert, a microbiologist, a veterinarian, a teacher, a museum designer and others. An assortment of personalities, from gregarious to taciturn.

Is it awkward, this reunion? Do we struggle to reconnect? Does conversation degenerate into embarrassing silences?

2016 is a Presidential election year and the political views of our group range from libertarian to liberal. Does friction ensue, arguments erupt, hostility surface to erode old friendships?

Many of us have come alone but others have brought wives or girlfriends. Does this create a social divide, a bifurcation of acceptable language and behavior?

Each of us is subject to the ravages of age, but in different ways and to different degrees. Do we assign weight to each degree of health and robustness, categorize and cull those greater or lesser able and avoid their contagion or seeming superiority?

To each of these questions the answer is a resounding no.

We are friends of half a century and for a few September days those years dissolve and Watermill Cove is transformed into 912 Elm. The mirror and our bodies argue otherwise but thru this weekend we are boys again, young & full of fun and foolishness. These may be Autumn days but they are bright with golden-hued laughter, mellow and gentle with a newfound appreciation for how rare and uncommon is the glow of the vintage friendship that surrounds us.

Man has been described as "the story-telling animal" and a sociobiologist would've found ample confirmation of that theory in our rustic villa by the lake. In more ways than one it was a storied weekend. Tales of our long-ago adventures and misadventures were re-assembled, cobbled together with the glue of a kind of group memory, one of us remembering part of an episode from the past, then others contributing their recollection of the event until the story became whole and complete. Here's one example, as contributed by Steve McD:

When I worked washing dishes at Stephens College (an exclusive girl's 'finishing school' in Columbia), I came to know several Suzies (the generic Stephens girl), some fairly well and some by name only. I often saw acquaintances standing on Stephens Corner by the phone booths and that gave me an idea: how 'bout I jot down the phone number of every booth and when someone I recognize is hanging around there chatting with friends, I race up the street to my room, call the phone booth and ask for the girl – by name?

It was a long shot, but the laughs should be worth the effort. So, some days or weeks later, Tom and I were driving by Stephens Corner on the way to our house when I spied a girl I knew only by name. We hurried to our house and I gave Tom the number and turned the whole endeavor over to him.

When a girl answered, Tom asked if Tiffany was there. As it turned out, our victim was the one who'd answered the phone. Tom, in some sort of smooth, sonorous voice that only he could pull off, launched into a conversation with her as if he knew her and calling her at the phone booth was perfectly normal.

It was one of the most comical things I've ever heard, but I suppose you had to be there to appreciate the full effect.

The stories told were more than remembrances of 912 Elm, though. Each of us has lived a life over the intervening fifty years and because we are friends, we wanted to learn how every life had unfolded.

Seventy-year-old men are not braggarts, at least not graduates of 912 Elm. Honesty and openness were in our voices, sometimes choked with emotion as successes intermingled with struggles and troubles, illness and foolishness, trial and error. Nor was any story met with other than understanding and acceptance. It's a rare life reaches seventy years without wobbles and worries. That's a lesson all have learned.

But we made it thru, and the reason why might lie in the single sound that most filled and defined this weekend even more than the munching of chips and other assorted snacks - the sound of good-humored laugher. Laugher for the most part at our own foibles. We were by any measure a rather goofy crew at 912 Elm, but it may well be that very goofiness that carried us thru the inevitable trials and turmoil that mark a human lifespan.

So inevitably our time together too soon drew to a close. The weekend came to an end, but before we parted, we drank a heartfelt toast to the family we'd become, and to lost members of that family. We raised a glass to time, to laughter and to the sweet salvation of leavened 912-style goofiness.

And yes, that which we are, we are.

National Rotate Your Socks Day

Although most Americans are aware of the need to regularly rotate their car tires, a new study indicates it is far more important to rotate your socks. The Spring edition of the *Journal of Complementary Foot and Hoof Care* reports that inattention to proper sock maintenance is responsible for a large number of seemingly unrelated ailments* (*see Note #1 for details*).

The study, which involved several men age 19 thru 75 and a corresponding number of somewhat younger women ** (*see Note #2*) revealed that most were unaware that socks, like shoes, are designed to be worn on either the right foot or the left. A small "R" or "L" is encoded on the heel of each sock to designate on which foot the sock should be worn. Incorrect sock placement is a leading cause of toe jam and stinky foot.

Of equal importance, at least once a year sock order must be reversed or serious consequences can ensue. The precise reason for Sock Order Disorder (SOD) is not currently known, but is believed to relate to the rotation of the Earth. Because most of us live our entire lives in either the northern or southern hemisphere, over a number of years the constant spinning of our planet in the same direction can lead to certain complex physical and behavioral syndromes described in technical medical terms as being "Twisted" or "Screwed Up." Annual sock rotation is thought to alleviate these problems or at least make it so that, really, you just don't care.

Based upon this study, Foot Fetishists International (FFI) has designated April 1 National Rotate Your Socks Day and encourages all right-thinking Americans to take the indicated action for health and hygiene reasons. In many communities, FFI plans to establish storefront clinics for those who prefer to leave their sock rotation to skilled professionals. For further information, go to www.SockItToMe.org, Like us on Facebook, click on our App,

Tweet us, Skype us, LinkedIn us, Pinterest us, hail a ride on uber or do the Hand Jive like Sister Flo.

* Note #1, Partial Listing of ailments which have been linked to improper sock maintenance:

Dizziness, slew foot, tinnitus, pigeon toe, moles, pimples, hangnails, lump jaw, licanthropy, heebie-jeebies, hitch in the giddyup, halitosis, purple haze, pollution of Precious Bodily Fluids, chortling, weeble-wobble, snarkiness, boogers, Lackanookie, toxic flatulence, line dancing, leakage, shenanigans, frumpiness, hankerings, Ramalama Ding-dong, rumble-gut, frog-face, thrips, zombieism, hey-nonny-nonny, dilithium crystals, fumble fingers, skinks, dishabile, blown gaskets, woolly-bully, waffle cone, subjunctives, wiggle-worm, wallabies, sharknados, flat-foot floogie with the floy-floy, hives, chives, Currier & Ives, low T, low T & A, rockin' pneumonia and boogie-woogie flu.

**Note #2, Female Study Subjects: The Dallas Cowboy cheerleaders

Waiting

I am waiting
Waiting for evening,
For the sun to slip low
And shadows sprawl
And the world to grow soft
As hymns.

This is the hour
When yesterdays come close
Calling
With wordless song
To follow
And never forget.

Here among the coolest colors
And quiet rustling of leaves
And souls
Is where the truth
And all answers rest

Tom Kiske

Waiting for you

Waiting for me

Even as I am waiting.

Sock it to *Me?*

In the mad midst of the Holiday shopping season, last week I found myself in serious need of socks. Almost my entire inventory of this essential item had been depleted one by one, the Holy Season having been preceded by a lengthy holey season during which ventilated socks had one-by-one been banished, never to return. Alas, the consequences of this disposal program had now reached crisis proportions.

Something must be done!

At this frantic time of year nothing short of a crisis would impel me to brave the hostile hordes shoving and elbowing their way thru equally pugnacious - tho relentlessly cheery - squadrons of competing shoppers doing battle over a dwindling supply of Perfect Christmas Gifts. Cruel fate had condemned me to venture into a region the stumpy Y chromosome leaves men ill-equipped to navigate - or survive!

Still, it was Winter and global warming hadn't yet reached the point where I could go sockless. Thus it was that I entered the battle zone that was WalMart (yes, Walmart) with both trepidation and determination. I'd strategized that an early morning assault on the objective might find opposing forces not yet at full strength, posing less risk of injury in the inevitable crossfire and fog of war. Quickly I scampered thru the aisles, hyper-alert to Incoming, dodging impatient shoppers hurtling my way, feinting and weaving to avoid a barrage of items flung willy-nilly from shelves in the general direction of a waiting shopping cart.

At last, there it was - the sock section. A rapid scan failed to reveal the easy choice I'd hoped for: the same socks I was used to. It seems socks now come in an endless variety, much like toothpaste and shampoo. I was close to panic realizing I'd failed to research which socks were "in" according to some Influencer. Then, realizing it was unlikely I'd find such prestigious footwear in a WalMart, I grabbed a pack that looked somewhat similar to my old ones and beat a hasty retreat from the field of battle.

It was a few days later that I tore into my new pack-o-socks. Imagine my surprise when I learned I was about to don what were described as "Performance Socks!"

Hmmm, I wondered, what kind of performance did these socks provide or enhance? The package offered no guidance, so I was left to speculate. Would I discover a previously unknown talent for tap dancing? For boot-scootin'? For leaping tall buildings in a single bound or at least a restored ability to dunk a basketball? Maybe my old record in the 100m would again be achievable? Wow - any of these would be great!

Sadly, a few experiments revealed no magic in these socks.

How disappointing!

Then for the first time I noticed what brand of socks it was I'd purchased. They were Dickies! Wait - I found these in the sock section, right? So surely, you're supposed to wear 'em on your *feet*, aren't you? But how could that . . .?

Still, they ARE performance socks. Worth a try, I guess.

Something Scary This Way Comes

I was in college before I saw an actual ghost, but long before that there were the stories. As kids we were surrounded by tales of the supernatural, not always ghosts, but a wild assortment of weird creatures whose sole purpose was to maim, kill or at least scare the bejeebers out of you. There were comic books like <u>The Crypt of Terror</u> and <u>The Vault of Horror</u>, radio programs like <u>The Inner Sanctum</u> and movies like <u>Frankenstein, Dracula, The Wolfman</u> and <u>Invaders from Mars</u>. There were vegetable "pods" that would dispose of you and take your place if you fell asleep. The Thing, the Creature, Them and even the gelatinous Blob were out to get you - especially if you were a teenager. Nor was school a refuge from bizarre threats, thanks to reading lists that included <u>The Tell-tale Heart, Dr. Jekyll & Mr. Hyde</u> and Sleepy Hollow's headless horseman.

The stories that really got to you, though, were the ones a friend told you, swearing they were true. Not just the Urban Myth legends like the hook on the couple's car door handle or the scraping noise on the car roof that turned out to be a kid who'd been hung from the tree they'd parked under, but hushed accounts of things that happened way too close to home.

It was my friend Bryan who one evening told me about his neighbor and her strange nightly visitor. Mrs. Kettle, he said, was a very religious woman who lived in an old two-story across the courtyard from his house. Before her, the house had belonged to a man with a wooden leg whose past was said to have included a life of crime, some of it violent. He'd grown old and died in the house not long before Mrs. Kettle bought it.

Her bedroom was on the second floor and the disquieting visits began her very first night in the house. It was around midnight when she heard someone on the old wooden staircase. "The sound was something like this," Bryan said, "Crea-ea-ea-ea-k . . . THUMP! Crea-ea-ea-ea-k . . . THUMP! Crea-ea-ea-k . . . THUMP!" Like a man - a man with a wooden leg - climbing the ancient stairway.

This continued night after night, frightening Mrs. Kettle and troubling her sleep. Then one night the eerie footsteps approached ever closer, all the way to the top of the stairway, down the hall to the bedroom, crea-ea-ea-ea-ea-k . . . THUMP! Crea-ea-ea-ea-k . . . THUMP!

Finally, as Mrs. Kettle lie there trembling, bedclothes drawn up to her neck, the bedroom door flew open! Terrified, she cried out, "What, in the name of God, do you want!"

Immediately, the footsteps stopped, never to return.

After hearing this story, I have to admit that for several nights before I fell asleep, I listened pretty closely for the sound of old pegleg creeping up on me, while rehearsing the phrase that banishes him. And I wonder if it wasn't that story and all the others that sensitized me, so that as a college student when that odd mist-like humanoid presence crossed my path as I walked the dirt road on the outskirts of Columbia late at night, I knew it for what it was - or at least what it might have been.

It's been said the reason people don't see fairies, ghosts, angels or spirits anymore is that we no longer believe in such things. Like Tinker Bell fading away until her substance was restored by the chants of "I believe, I believe, I believe!" If you don't believe something's possible, how could you see it?

And so, if you have occasion to walk the halls of some lonely building late at night, be alert to what revenants might lurk there. Especially if you descend the stairs to the basement, listen closely for eerie echoes of long-silent voices, the faint sobs of lost souls, the hoarse and muffled warnings of restless and tormented entities. Basements are much favored by haunts and all sorts of unsettling goings-on, as I learned as a boy.

The basement in my parents' house was a fun place to play during daylight hours. Once the sun went down, though, it was transformed into something far more sinister. This was made worse by the fact there was only one light fixture suspended from the ceiling down there, with no switch controlling it. Instead, you carefully and worriedly went down the old wooden staircase in the dark, walked through the blackness to the middle of the room, then pulled the chain to turn on the light, wary of what it might reveal.

So, one unfortunately memorable night, down I go into what seemed the first level of hell, a trek anyone wishing to bathe was required to undertake to ignite the old galvanized water heater. As I cross to the dangling light bulb, I brush against something . . . feathery. This can't be right. Can't be good. I quickly yank the chain only to see right beside me a goose or duck or some other fowl creature hanging upside-down and headless from a clothes line, blood dripping from its neck into a stainless-steel bucket already half full of red gore. AAAARRRRGGGGHHHH!

Only later was it explained to a shivering, permanently scarred young Tom, that our Polish upstairs neighbors were preparing chanina, duck blood soup. Apparently this is a delicacy in Poland, upstairs in our house, and no doubt in Transylvania.

My advice: avoid basements, closed-off, boarded-up rooms, and other places where traces of long-ago events linger and evil claws across the floor, slobbering and eager to feed upon the living. Not to mention the possibility you might stumble across a decapitated duck dripping blood.

Stay in well-lit places. Stay in the company of cheerful, happy friends. Hostile, unseen forces and bizarre recipes inhabit the darkness.

Beware! Beware!

Tom Kiske

Spare Girl

St. Louis. 1960-something. A warm summer night. I'm driving out Broadway going - somewhere. Anywhere. It's a warm summer night and I'm a young man. Windows down, the wind feels good in my face. In my hair. I'm just - looking. Searching. Feeling my way. Am I going towards something, or away? What strange force keeps me moving?

A car pulls alongside me but doesn't pass. Matches speed. We travel together a minute or two. I glance over. Convertible. A bunch of kids my age. Driver yells over, *"Hey, she needs a guy,"* gestures to a girl in the backseat with another couple. They have a spare girl.

"She needs a guy," isn't so much a statement as a question. I signal my thumbs-up.

"Follow us," the guy yells.

We end up at a little park next to Jefferson Barracks, the one with the carousel. One of the guys introduces me to Spare Girl. She acts embarrassed at the circumstances, but she's not *too* embarrassed.

Couples wander off into the darkness.

Spare Girl and I talk softly in the night. For a while we sit together atop a playground sliding board. How the conversation goes is lost to me now - what school, do you know so-and-so, that kind of thing, probably. It doesn't much matter. Spare Girl likes me. Not because of my sparkling repartee, I'm sure. I'm a quiet guy. What is it then? The way I look? That I seem "nice?" That she's alone, in need of company and I just happen to fall within some range of acceptability?

Spare Girl smokes. Lights a cigarette, offers it to me. Do I take a puff? I don't remember, but probably. Being polite. Being nice.

Spare Girl is getting drawn in, sits closer.

After a while the other kids return. They want to go to this nightclub on Chippewa. I know the place. There's a dental office there today.

I'm not much interested in going.

I'm not much interested in Spare Girl.

She's cute enough, she's clearly interested in me, but by some obscure, ill-defined mental or emotional mating mathematics I've ruled her out. Don't want this to go any further.

I manufacture an excuse. I have to go home and change clothes. Meet you at the club later.

She senses what's up. "You don't need to change," she tells me, "You're fine."

But I want out.

Everything in the universe is flying apart from everything else. Gravity isn't strong enough to hold things together. Whatever force is at work here in the park tonight isn't strong enough either. I'm leaving. My blind, fumbling search has found no answer here.

"It'll just be a few minutes," I lie, "I'll meet you there."

I drive off. We both know we'll never see each other again.

* * *

Fifty years later I wonder, does Spare Girl remember that warm summer night? Probably not, but if so, *how* does she remember it?

How did her life turn out? Did she marry? Is she now a St. Louis housewife, 2.5 children perhaps? Was that night her only romantic disappointment or merely one in a series?

And on warm summer nights now do her thoughts sometimes return to the park? Does she wonder what became of me? Does she wonder about what might have been, what formless future drove off long ago with that strange, quiet young man?

I Have Found Sunlight

I have found sunlight
Playing among the thunderheads,
Deep shadow specters
In summer afternoons.
I've smelled the rain
Before it fell,
Heard the whisper
Haunted yesterdays tell.
I climbed and fallen and gained snow summits,
Dived deeper than my breath,
Seeking something once I desperately knew,
Too sweet to linger on the tongue,
Too light for Earth's mean gravity.
More than a dream it was.
It was
More solid than this rock, my chambered heart
But somewhere gone I follow
'Til all strengths fail and I am called
To sunlight through this passing storm.
To sunlight that finds me.

What Lurks in your Fridge?

Last Saturday morning I opened my refrigerator and inside was ... a little man! He was a *very* little man, no larger than the nub of a well-used pencil, but nicely dressed in a tiny blue pin-striped suit, a red and white tie and a yellow hard hat. He seemed as startled to see me as I was him.

"Uh, good morning," he said with a shy little smile, "How are you today?"

"OK, I guess," I replied, "But who *are* you and why are you, you know, *in my fridge*?

"I'm Bob." he said, "I work here."

"You work in my fridge?"

"I do, but really, you're not supposed to see me. I kinda messed up."

"How'd that happen?" I asked.

"Well, it was last night – Friday night. You had that wine in here and I mighta overindulged a bit."

"You drank my wine?"

"Oh, you'll never miss it," he said, "After all, I'm a little man, so it only takes a little swig to get me schnockered."

"Makes sense, I suppose, but you still haven't explained what you do in here, aside from getting tanked on Friday nights."

The little man leaned against a milk carton, furrowed his tiny brow and thought very hard for a minute, then grinned and said," I make sure your fridge is cold so your food is safe."

"Well, I definitely want my fridge cold and my food safe," I said, "but since when does it take a ... a..."

"A little man?" he prompted.

"Yes. Why's it take a little man to keep the fridge cold?"

"Good question," he said. "See, these new refrigerators are way more complicated than the older models. Even the compressor's

133

different. It's not just on or off like they used to be. Now it's got different speeds. And of course, everything's computerized."

"Wow, I had no idea. So, you're trained on running all this stuff?"

"Trained?" he scoffed, "I have a Master's degree in Cold Engineering from MIT. They are quite accommodating to the stature-impaired; got a whole campus set up on a table top there in Cambridge."

"My goodness," I said, "Does the job pay well?"

"Well enough. Plus, you know, all the snacks and drinks I can, uh, *sample*."

"Right. But you have to work in the dark, don't you? I mean once the fridge door is closed ..."

"Black as a moonless night in the country," he agreed, "but I have a flashlight and these little-bitty night vision goggles. It's not so bad when you get used to it."

"But don't you get chilly?"

"Nah." he said, "Thermal underwear. Also, as I may have mentioned, you get used to things."

"Intriguing." I said, "Listen, you think I could come inside there? Just for a minute or so to see what it's like?"

"Come on, use your head," Bob gibed, "We're a bit tight on space in here and you're not a, uh..."

"A little man?" I suggested.

"Exactly. Besides, I really have to get to work before things go all cattywhumpus."

"Sure. I understand, but one more question, ok?"

"Shoot," he said agreeably.

"I've noticed sometimes the temperature in the fridge varies unpredictably. Why is that?"

"Yeah," Bob answered, "Sometimes it's just the cycle the fridge happens to be on when you open it. It runs self- tests and stuff. Also, maybe the compressor's on a slow cycle."

"Hmmm."

"Then, too, sometimes I kinda mess with you."

"What? Hey!"

"Listen, close the door, ok? You're letting all the cold air out. Makes my job way more difficult. Get what you need, get out, close the door, let me work."

"OK, OK, don't get all huffy," I said.

"Bye-bye."

I closed the door, finished my breakfast and headed in to the office. I mentioned my morning encounter with the little man to a few co-workers, but they just looked at me funny, so I decided to pretty much keep it to myself.

A few days later, on a hunch I jerked the fridge door open really quickly hoping to catch Bob again. No little man in the fridge this time, though. Just a tiny sign reading "Out to Lunch."

I never spotted Bob again, but once in while on a Saturday morning, if I've left a bottle of wine in the fridge the night before it seems a tiny bit short.

Suffering

Q: Why is there suffering in the world?

The authors of the Bible and Biblical scholars have wrestled with this problem literally for thousands of years. The answers they've proposed are termed "theodicies," (a term coined by Gottfried Leibniz in the 17th Century) but none satisfy because all are incompatible with the concept of an omnipotent, omniscient and loving God.

Here's my theodicy:

Why is there suffering in the world?

There isn't.

"In the world" there are merely things that happen. Suffering takes place in the mind, in the "heart" or in the soul.

Is suffering then exclusively a human condition? Does the gazelle taken down by a lion suffer, or the wildebeest in the jaws of a crocodile? Certainly, these creatures feel pain, and to that degree they may be said to suffer, but it seems clear that only in humans is the capacity for suffering fully developed. We can suffer for "psychological" reasons, from "emotional abuse," and we can suffer for others.

The lion and crocodile almost certainly do not "suffer" because of the pain they inflict - were they to do so they would probably be unsuccessful in their assigned role as predator. More, tho, the gazelle herd, the wildebeest herd likely suffer little if anything in the face of the pain of one of their fellows.

Human beings have the uncommon, if not unique, trait of empathy. An Asian tsunami, a Haitian earthquake, a children's cancer ward, all touch our hearts and we "feel the pain" of those directly affected. We suffer vicariously.

If such be the case, the initial question must be modified. It is not "why is there suffering in the world," but rather, "why do humans have this pronounced capacity to experience suffering?"

Some might argue it is this very capacity which also enables us to feel happiness, that without pain there can be no joy. Not so. What may be true is that one cannot fully *appreciate* his happy state without having experienced its opposite, but the emotion of joy does not require having first felt pain, any more than one need not have first experienced joy to know pain.

It is possible, tho, that at least some forms of human suffering require knowledge - or belief - that a different state is possible. Children do not *have to* starve, or be abused. Homes do not *have to* be built in flood-prone areas. Automobiles *can* be made to keep their occupants safe in a crash. Slavery *can* be abolished. We *can* do something to alleviate suffering.

WE can. We don't have to wait for God to do it, we can help. We can build a better world. Maybe, given enough time, intelligence and effort, we can construct an approximation of The Kingdom of God right here.

And if we CAN help those who suffer, but fail to do so, is this not tantamount, in Biblical terms, to a sin?

Does sin exist within the human heart?

Does God?

Was Jesus trying to teach not about some mythological deity in the sky, but one that can be developed from the human heart?

Alternative Dentistry

When a tooth began bothering me, I decided to bypass my regular dentist, who continues to rely on old-fashioned measures like drilling, filling cavities and preventive oral hygiene and care. I'd heard so much about wonderful new treatments available through "alternative dentistry" that I resolved to give it a try. I made an appointment with Dr. Peter Thomas Barnum, a graduate of the Leeward Island School of Holistic Dentistry and Good Feelings.

As I drove up for my visit, I noticed that Dr. Barnum doesn't operate out of a traditional dentist's "office," but rather in a modest frame residence in an older and, uh, less affluent part of town. I rang the doorbell somewhat timorously, thinking perhaps I had the wrong address. A harried woman carrying a squalling infant in each arm opened the door. When I asked for Dr. Barnum, she grunted and directed me through to a small back bedroom.

Dr. Barnum, who appeared to have been dozing, leapt up from the bed as I entered and shook my hand vigorously. "Welcome, welcome," he said, "This is first visit, no?"

"Uh, yes," I replied, glancing about in vain for a dental chair and the usual equipment.

"Please, you sit there," Dr. Barnum said, pointing to a large, well-worn easy chair. From a small table nearby, a thin wisp of incense curled upward.

"Gosh, it's kinda dark in here," I said, noticing that the blinds were drawn, so that the room was lit only by a few votive candles.

"Bright light no good for teeth," Dr. Barnum answered, "No lightbulb in mouth, eh?"

"I suppose not."

"Fer sure. Now, you tell doctor why you come here today."

"I think I have a cavity in my second molar," I said.

"Ach, molar schmolar," scoffed Dr. Barnum, "No sciency stuff. Tell me feeling!

"Well," I said, "it feels like the tooth hurts."

"Yes, yes," Doctor Barnum smiled, "pain can be many problems. You are anxious, maybe? Tired but not sleeping?"

"Well, the toothache makes it a little tough to sleep"

"Mmm-hmmm," Dr. Barnum nodded, narrowing his eyes, "How 'bout chewing? You pay attention how you chew?"

"How I chew? Well, I guess maybe I try to avoid that tooth."

"Ha! So!" Is problem!" the doctor exclaimed triumphantly. "You breathe in when chew, or out?"

I had to think about that for a minute. "Gosh," I said, "I really don't know."

"*Big* problem. People too busy," Dr. Barnum said, "No time. Chewing and breathing work together goodly or badly." He handed me a small blue crystal. "Hold over head," he commanded.

"Huh? What's this supposed to do?"

"Calcium channel crystal," he explained, "Focuses galactic enamel rays on dental chakra."

"Oh," I said, raising the crystal over my head.

"Here, I think," he mumbled, moving my hand as if to position the crystal in a certain spot. "Now," he went on, "you practice: breathe in, chew; breathe out, swallow."

I tried it a few times, biting down as I inhaled, and trying to exhale as I swallowed. It wasn't easy.

"Good, good," grinned the doctor, "be sure to masturbate food, like Kama Sutra says."

"Um, don't you mean masticate?"

Dr. Barnum's grin widened, "No, Grasshopper. Must get food aroused, make joyous. Unhappy food pollutes precious bodily fluid, rots toothies."

"Precious ... say, isn't that from Doctor Strangelove?"

"Who is strangelover doctor? Maybe he's copying me. I don't like that. Maybe I'll sue. You know a good lawyer?"

"Uh, listen, never mind," I said, "what about my toothache?"

"Ah, yes." Dr. Barnum waved an open beaker of foul-smelling greenish liquid under my nose. "Take a big ol' whiff!"

I did as I was told. "Urrgh," I gagged, "what the heck *is* that?"

"Aromatherapy," he explained. "Latest thing. Essence of tooth decay, by Estee Laudenum. Body has to learn aversion to tooth stink."

"Uh-huh, OK, but what about the pain?"

"Poo! Pain is fignewton of imagination. Go to happy place, calm place. Maybe pretty creek or beach or waterfall place you like."

"OK, I'm thinking of California beach," I said.

"Fine, fine. Now think pain is driftwood floating off, floating away," the doctor whispered, slowly waving his arms with his eyes closed, swaying like a hula dancer.

"I'm trying," I protested, "but couldn't you just do a filling or something? This thing really hurts.

The doctor frowned. "You are not co-operating!" he said, clearly upset I'd interrupted his hula. "Come here, lay on bed. On belly."

I got up from the easy chair and flopped onto the bed as he'd asked. Doctor Barnum pounced on me and began vigorously massaging and pummeling my back.

"Doc, what're you doing now? I demanded.

"You got subluxation of third vertebrae, squeezes toothal nerve. I gotta adjust."

"Geeze," I whimpered, "could you maybe adjust a little softer? I'm getting bruises."

"Don't be a sissy-boy!" Doctor Barnum bellowed, grabbing my head with both hands and giving it an abrupt twist, "There! Now you're all better. Get up. Pay now. Go home. Be happy fella."

"I staggered groggily toward the door. "Is that it? What about my tooth?"

"Keep crystal over head for week. Let dental rays work. That'll be $125."

"$125? But my tooth still hurts, dammit!"

Dr. Barnum grabbed a small bottle from a wooden cabinet, shoved it in my hand. "Take a pill twelve time every day. Come back in a week. $55 more."

"Huh? What kinda pills are these?"

"Dr. Barnum's special formula happy tooth vitamin – got melatonin, amdro, phen-phen and little bit Cheez-Whiz. Good for you. Don't ask so many questions. Go home. Sit in dark room. Listen soft music. Play nicknack on paddywack. You feel better."

"Soft music ..."

"Sure," Doctor Barnum said, "No Celine Dion, tho. That screetchy voice can crack your teeth. Also, keep crystal on head. Pay now."

I started writing a check with my right hand, holding the crystal in place with my left.

"Cash and carry, please," said the doctor, "no check, no credit card, no paypal crap."

I counted out the money. "What should I do if the tooth gets worse, doc?'

"I dunno," he said, "Pray. Maybe a tooth angel will come. Bye-bye, now."

Later that evening when the pain intensified, I resorted to my own form of alternative dentistry with a length of string and a doorknob. Not as mystical, touchy-feely and new age as the methods of Dr. Barnum and other alternative practitioners, perhaps, but quick, effective and less expensive.

I'm still a little worried about my precious bodily fluids, though.

Note: An early version of this story appeared first in the January, 2000 issue of <u>Informensa</u>.

Solace

So cold and dark
Comes 2 a.m.
Where empty and alone
I know
My sorry, naked self
The gift I've squandered.
The punishment I've earned.

Yet by the morning
Light, I've wrought
My shame and sins
Into these thin words

And thus shielded
By my pen
And paper god

I go on.
I go on.

The Cold Front

A weather-troubled morning. Heavy gray clouds cover most of the angry sky, settling over it like a dark cap worn at a rakish angle. The wind picks up, straight and strong from the north. Flags snap to attention. Trees, fresh with Spring's green growth, dance gracefully in susurrant rhythm.

A strange excitement spreads among us, stirring feelings that live in the deepest parts of us, lingering from ancient days when we dwelled in nature and with nature instead of above it and against it. A remnant of some old apprehension arises in the chest, throws off the smothering blanket of reasoned articulation and whispers in the old tongue, "Beware – danger approaches."

We're pack animals, herd animals. Signs in nature invisible to our higher functions spook us. We grow skittish without knowing why or what to do.

And so, schooled by a thousand or more years of civilization, we ignore our feelings, scoff and laugh nervously at our fears, and in striving to rise above instinct and passions and ways of knowing not reducible to words and formulae, we sacrifice the secret signing of the soul.

The Sky at Morning

A cool 65 degrees greeted me the morning of August 27, 2015 as I stumbled outside to fetch the newspaper from the driveway. A spectacular sunrise illuminated the sky in blue and pink pastels. A scene of such scale can't be captured in a photograph. I've tried many times, only to be disappointed by a picture inadequate to the task of capturing what my eyes had seen.

A sunrise like that lights not only the sky, but *everything*. Ordinary surroundings acquire a mystic glow. You want to preserve the magic, but within moments the light and colors change, fade, dissipate and are gone. Despite the pixel count of the camera phone, it's embarrassingly puny confronted with a task of the morning's majesty. You may take a picture, but it isn't what you saw, what you experienced. The scene stirred feelings, drama and a sense of the spiritual. A photo does none of that.

Perhaps it's the very transitory nature of sunrise and sunset that imbues them with such emotional content. We hear whispered cautions that our own allotted span is brief as well. We're reminded of the importance of pausing to savor the moment and the immeasurable value of simple things.

When the end comes, I suspect I'll recall little of the accumulated months and years of driving to work, of a trainload of problems that seemed crucial and urgent at the time, of national and international crises that dominated news media, of political campaigns and rivalries that manufactured issues to divide and confuse us.

But I hope I will remember that one morning I stepped outside half asleep to get the paper and was awakened by the sky; the grandeur and glory of the solemn sky.

The Kitchen Window

The one on the right.
Summer, it held the window fan
Which blew hot air outward.
Crack the bedroom window,
The theory went,
Cooler air was drawn in.
Not really much cooler, but
At least a breeze.
Better at bedtime.

When Winter came
The fan was put away and
Sometimes the window was lifted
To cool an apple pie resting on the
sill,
Hot from my mother's oven.

The black dial phone
Stood silent sentinel on a small table
By the window,
Waiting quietly with me
In case the girl would call.

Sometimes a generous God
Awarded me the sweet, soft voice
Of that young girl, who phoned to say

Tom Kiske

She liked me

And I would feel warm inside
As just-baked pie.

The Lamp

"If I were a carpenter
And you were a lady . . ."

Tim Hardin

Sometimes you look in the mirror and wonder how you became the person reflected there. For me, part of the answer goes back to seventh grade. Back then, boys in that grade had to take a course in "manual training." We shortened it to simply "manual."

Humboldt School had no shop so one day a week we walked the few miles to Shephard School. We were allowed ample time to get there, so the trip itself became an adventure. I walked with my friends, Bill, William and Jimmy. Having neither smart phones nor apps we made up our own games to amuse ourselves along the way, from leaping off retaining walls to exploring vacant lots along the route. And we discussed things important to the adolescent mind, one of which was growing in importance.

Girls.

"What do you think they do while we're at manual?" Jimmy asked one day.

Good question. None of us had actually ever talked to a girl, mysterious and somewhat frightening creatures that they were. "I don't know," Bill confessed, "Maybe play with dolls?"

William had a sister. In our minds this was not quite the same as an actual girl, but we figured it gave him a leg up on the rest of us. "I don't think 7th grade girls still play with dolls," he advised, "Probably they just take a nap or something."

Remarkably, half a century would elapse before a Humboldt/McKinley girl enlightened me about what they really did. They learned how to cook, sew, make a bed, set a proper table and perhaps most critically, they learned the rules of etiquette.

147

Remember, gender roles were set in concrete in the 50's. Nobody ever asked a girl if she'd like to take manual, or a boy if he might enjoy cooking. Such questions would've been an affront to "community standards."

So, it was off to manual we boys went each week. Mr. Blight was the teacher. He was a tall, slender man with a slight limp and a way about him that was both gentle and firm. He quickly earned our respect, no mean feat as like most boys our age we were no more than little heathens and potential hoodlums, as evidenced by the big "rumble" that happened one day between the Shephard boys and we Humboldt ruffians - about which the less said the better. It was *not* a scene from "West Side Story."

And Mr. Blight was not like most teachers. What he taught was far different from other classes where you might, for example, read about the principal export of Guatemala. Instead, we learned about tools. And about woodworking. We learned the difference between a cross-cut saw and a rip saw. We found out what a brace and bit were and how to use a wood plane without chipping or splitting the end of the piece. We learned how to use and take care of tools, how to square up a piece of lumber, what it meant to chamfer a board and how to approach a project in a methodical, step by step fashion. We got none of this from a book. Mr. Blight <u>showed</u> us. We learned from his quiet, patient example.

For the end of the semester, we were to put our newfound knowledge to work by actually making something. Like many of my friends, my project was a pump lamp. It was not a simple endeavor. You had to follow directions and do things right or it wouldn't turn out. There was measuring and sawing and drilling and some delicate work with a chisel. The components had to be properly joined. There was sanding and staining and finishing. It involved wood and plastic and some basic electric wiring as well. It was work, but it was fun, too. And Mr. Blight was nearby to offer help where needed.

I messed up a little. Misread one dimension for the pump handle and made a poor choice of plastic color. Still, I made a serviceable lamp. Not perfect, but good enough to grace my parents' night stand for many years. Since their passing the pump lamp sits on my desk. The Manual project still casts its light after more than fifty years.

When we walked into Mr. Blight's shop, we were boys. We learned from him how to do things. Practical skills we would put to use for the rest of our lives. We had become makers of things and by extension fixers of broken things. We had mastered some beginning steps on the road to becoming men, as men were seen in the 1950's.

And as I look back on it, we benefitted from what the girls were taught as well. Not right then and not directly, but later by a sort of osmosis - because of the way a woman has of chamfering, smoothing the edges of the rough-hewn man she chooses, instilling in him an appreciation for a nuanced world apart from the aggressive, unruly male culture. If Mr. Blight's coaching helped make men of us, what the girls learned while we were off at manual, in time made us better men. Made us husbands and fathers.

And now as evening approaches, I wonder if even today the way we see ourselves and the world around us is in the light that lingers from the lamps and lessons of our youth.

The Poetry Inside

"The poet speaks on behalf of the least tangible, but also possibly deepest, awareness that we possess. But it's an awareness so elusive, so fitful in its arrivals, that we mainly live in forgetfulness. The poem is a memory flash of a meaning that exceeds us, that hovers almost completely out of our reach. Poetry is an intrusion, an over-and-above that sets almost everything else for the moment at naught."

Sven Birkets, "The German Poet" in <u>The Other Walk</u>

Words have the power to induce transcendence.

Is there not a kind of minor miracle in this simple truth? Men did not always possess the gift of speech, of words. Language is a capacity evolved over thousands or even millions of years, no doubt originating as a tool of survival.

Now we have honed that tool to the point we can employ it to re-connect with that elemental force from which our other implements and artifacts have left us distant and isolated.

There are other avenues, of course, by which we seek to remind ourselves that the physical world we inhabit is no more than one expression of a vastly greater cosmos, of forces and influences at once immense and subtle – and far beyond our human ken. Music, religion, art and even nature's own visions and vistas whisper to us that we have inside; something from somewhere else. Something that joins us with all of Creation: that which we see and hear and touch, and that larger sphere we too rarely feel. Something that is a kind of glowing poetry that lives inside each of us from birth.

Something a little lost and lonely, but always reaching out and up.

The Other Raven

(With apologies to Edgar Allen Poe)

Once upon a midnight dreary, I couldn't sleep, my eyes were
bleary
From reading volumes of forgotten lore
While I nodded, nearly farting, suddenly there came a barking
I'm gonna kill them dogs next door.

Argh, how stinky I remember, passing gas that bleak December
Those dogs I will dismember so that they shall bark no more
Eagerly I wished for quiet, hoped that maybe I could buy it
Thought at least I had to try it
Still those dogs outside did roar

Surely, I must be a klutz, enduring them there lousy mutts
No, it's time to kick their butts, and this will be my chore
I will grab them by the tail
And then you'll surely hear 'em wail
For I'll whup 'em til they're sore.

But alas, I fear I blew it, for my spouse said 'you can't do it'
(All along I think she knew it) as I walked across the floor
They're our neighbors, after all
And their dogs we cannot maul
Tho the darn things make a racket
We must find a way to hack it.

Quoth the raven, 'Nevermore.'

𝕵ending

"Tending the Mountain" is the title of a New Age song by Ruth Cunningham. Like much of the music of this genre, it's peaceful, relaxing to the mind. I think that when the human mind relaxes it's like a muscle unclenching. It loosens, opens up, expands. Tension is relieved and for a time you see things a little differently.

Does a mountain require tending? What does tending the mountain mean?

It could be taken to mean something akin to grooming, I suppose. In the case of Camelback Mountain in Phoenix, for example, you might tend the mountain by policing the trails, cleaning up debris left behind by thoughtless climbers. You'd be prettying up old Camelback.

But that's not the way I see it.

I think tending the mountain implies something more like paying attention to it. Seeing it. Recognizing it. Considering it. Perhaps not to the extent of worshipping it as certain native American tribes might, but at least affording it a measure of respect. I do not believe a mountain is a god, but surely it is God's handiwork.

Too often in today's world we tend to view things in terms of their utility. What *good* is this thing? To what *use* can it be put? A river is not simply a river, but a potential source of hydroelectric power or cheap transportation or alluvial deposits to nourish our crops. A forest can be harvested for timber. The ground beneath our feet can be tapped for coal and oil and gas to fuel our busy lives.

But what good is a mountain?

Well, it could be transformed into a giant sculpture life Mount Rushmore to draw tourist dollars, or if it's big enough a snowpack could provide skiing in Winter and fresh meltwater in Springtime.

But maybe it's enough for a mountain to just be a mountain, like a soul is just a soul.

And maybe at times both need tending.

The Shameful Towel Incident

I don't know how many St. Louis grade schools had a Bath Day, but at my school, Humboldt, there was a weekly Bath Day.

Many today will be surprised that until a law was passed in the late 40's, many homes in the Soulard area lacked indoor plumbing. Backyards had a little facility with a half-moon cut-out in the door. Taking care of business was an experience few looked forward to. Not only do outhouses stink, they also attract a million or so bugs, most of which delight in buzzing around your face. If you didn't have a toilet, you likely also lacked a bath tub or shower. Instead, you dragged a metal tub into the kitchen and filled it from the sink. In winter you boiled water for a tepid bath. Afterward, you had to figure out how to empty the tub. It was a pain.

So, if you went to Humboldt, you just waited for Bath Day. It was actually shower day, but we called it Bath Day. We had a bath teacher, Miss Holman. I don't think she was actually a teacher, more like a matron or something but that term wasn't in our limited vocabulary, so even though she didn't teach anything – we weren't stupid; we knew how to use soap and water – we still called her the bath teacher.

Miss Holman's main job was to make sure we stood in an orderly line on the way to the showers, and – this was very important – to ensure we all stepped thru the tray of milky water. Nobody ever told us what that solution was, but we figured it must've been for athlete's foot. That was never confirmed, tho, so it might've just been something Miss Holman concocted to bolster her job description.

Picture this: a line of scrawny grade school boys naked except for towels wrapped around their middles, waiting to step thru the milk tray and into the showers. It's next to the boiler in the Humboldt basement and it's always steamy and hot. We trudge forward one at a time. There's no laughing or cutting up. Miss Holman is strict. She had to be or things could quickly get out of hand. Like what happened to me.

At that tender age I was a bashful kid, didn't much like standing around nearly naked in front of a strange woman. Then one day it got worse. I'm not sure if the kid behind me yanked my towel or if I just hadn't tied it tight enough, but it slipped off, dropped to the floor. And Miss Holman saw it! Beheld me in all my pre-adolescent glory. Humboldt's own living, breathing David, if not in exactly Michelangelo's perfect proportions.

Was Miss Holman understanding, sympathetic to my obvious embarrassment? Did she calmly suggest I retrieve my towel and move along? Alternatively, did she gaze appreciatively on my revealed manhood, perhaps mutter a lustful "Wow?"

Heck no. The woman was irate! Furious!

"YOU!" she screeched, "I don't want to see that!" You cover yourself right now!"

I froze. Nobody had ever yelled at me like that. I think I went into shock. My brain stopped working. My body stopped working. I was naked *and* paralyzed while Miss Holman grew more and more agitated. She waved her arms around in a frenzy. Hopped up and down. Spittle flew from her frothing mouth. She may have even yelled some bad words, but by then all I heard was an inarticulate buzzing. A very loud, very angry buzzing directed at poor timid Tommy! What should I do? In my thoroughly confused pre-adolescent mind, I thought maybe when she said "I don't want to see that," what she might've meant was "Wowee, I wanna see more of that!" I acted accordingly.

Fortunately, before things got worse, before Miss Holman called the vice squad, my friend Bill picked up my towel and wordlessly handed it to me. Mechanically, I re-tied it and things slowly returned to a semblance of normal, except for Miss Holman's bright red face and dagger-like stare. I hurried into the shower, dried off and fled the scene.

Needless to say, the story of the Towel Scandal spread quickly thru Humboldt school. Boys guffawed, girls giggled, teachers acted aloof from the whole tawdry affair but I knew they knew. Kind of a hard thing for a kid to live down, especially after being permanently banned from Bath Day. But after many years of intensive therapy . . .

Today, looking back on the incident from the distance of many decades, I suppose for all her Victorian outrage it strikes me maybe Miss Holman really was a teacher. After all, she taught me a lesson I never forgot. These days, I keep my towel tied really, really tight.

There's been wind all day.
I watch as the young Elm,
framed in the French doors,
Dances its supplication;
As the Spring-fresh leaves
Gather an oblique light
At once soft and specular,
So soon to dim, the sun sinking into
The last light, in Polish spoken as "Sha-da Go-
jeehna."
My mother recalling her mother's words
Long ago, but
Lingering,
As another day
Slips gently from now to memory.

𝕿𝖍𝖊 𝕾𝖊𝖛𝖊𝖓𝖘

*"You get old and you realize
there are no answers, just stories."*
Garrison Keillor

Years ago, at my high school when you reached the first semester of your senior year you were presented a "7" button, signifying your seventh semester, somewhat of a signal achievement. When I hit my seventh decade on this planet, I felt that was perhaps even more of an accomplishment, but did any organization award me a button or pin? Did I at least get some kind of ribbon? No. What I got was old.

Such a great gulf separates 70 from 17. Literally a lifetime. In so many ways we are no longer who we once were. Why then do we so often find ourselves looking back on our school days? Why do we read the newsletter, attend luncheons and reunions?

To some extent, of course, just because it's fun. Our memories are mostly fond ones. Lasting friendships were formed, adventures were undertaken, lessons learned, challenges met, laughter shared. Maybe we reminisce too as a form of escape. Aging can be a sobering experience, robbing us of energy, appearance and capability, inflicting aches physical & emotional. No wonder we want to return to a time when in Tennyson's words, "we were that strength which in old days moved earth and heaven."

But if that's all our visits back to school days are, they'd be no more than the mental equivalent of an old movie or TV show playing on the screen of our minds. <u>American Graffiti</u>, perhaps, or <u>The Many Loves of Dobie Gillis</u>. Entertaining, nostalgic, but devoid of deeper import.

I believe something far more important is going on when we reflect on Fast Times at You-Name-It High. Something that goes to the heart of what it means to be human. Socrates once proclaimed the unexamined life is not worth living and it may be that as we sift through our memories and re-tell the stories of our youth, as we share again our sometimes silly, sometimes sad adolescent episodes, as we examine them from an adult perspective, we transform a disjointed, disconnected jumble of individual days & deeds into a more cohesive sense of who we are and how we fit into the universe.

Thomas Moore says youthful experiences don't just come and go; they happen and then stay with us, continuing to "play out as important themes in our very identity." When we left high school to continue our education or launch careers and families our lives became busy and hectic. We were focused on the future and had little time to think of the past. Now as elders though, it seems our minds naturally turn back to when we were kids. As we call up events from earlier days, turn them over in our minds and discuss them with classmates, we're drawing stones from the stream of time, polishing them smooth so that they become gem-like we sometimes see facets we missed before in our impatient rush toward tomorrow.

There's an inescapable irony in the fact that now, when our supply of tomorrows is limited, we find we still have much to learn from our yesterdays. We 7's may be less active, but maybe we're more contemplative. We are growing not just older but deeper as well, so that as we mentally walk yesterday's well-known halls again patterns begin to emerge and we come to understand how the contours of the human spirit were molded by those long-ago events, friendships, and feelings.

It doesn't always happen. It doesn't happen for all of us, and when it does it's seldom an instantaneous flash of insight. It's not an "Aha!" moment. Instead, it's a slow shifting of perspective. Perhaps Matthew Arnold said it best:

"(you) see the world from a height, with prophetic eyes and a heart profoundly stirred, and face the fullness of the past."

It's a gradual dawning, a whisper that feels as if it comes from the center of things, revealing the shape and texture and hue of an entire lifetime, leaving us with a sense of wonder at the immense, evolving universe in which each of us plays a small but indispensable role.

In this way you may come to see you're not so different after all from that 17-year-old you once were. To age, after all, doesn't mean you lose all the other ages you used to be. And when you find that unaltered center, that calm and changeless core within, it could be that you've caught a glimpse of the pulsing perimeter of the human soul.

And I wonder, in our moments of silent reflection, with the smiles our memories bring, are we in some subtle way preparing for our final graduation? If so, I don't look upon it as a somber occasion. With any luck we'll be with our friends and maybe this time instead of trudging down the aisle to that stodgy old "Pomp & Circumstance" dirge, we'll be grooving to The Diamonds, stroh-oh-oh-lin' across the floor. "Fe-e-e -ls so good, take me by my hand . . .."

Tracks

The train came up on me unexpected. I'd been taking pictures of an old wooden railroad bridge over a small creek. I was walking up an unfinished road, exchanged "good morning's" with two workmen who were removing concrete forms along the road. I was thinking about how nice a cup of coffee would be when I heard the rumble of steel wheels on steel rails. It's a low-pitched rhythm like rolling thunder, but louder, closer, more insistent. More than hearing it, you *feel* it thrumming in your chest.

The train was making good time on a long, straight run. It sped quickly into view and then was abreast of me: three locomotives pulling a quarter mile run of freight and tank cars. Many of the cars were marked with artwork from the spray can of some anonymous artist defying authority in a far away rail yard, trying to say, as all artists must, I was here and this is my vision; *look.*

Three blasts from the engineer's whistle warned other travelers as the train approached a crossing. The pitch of the whistle dopplered into lower registers as the train receded into the distance, following the tracks to some southern destination unknown to we who watch.

There is a multifold mystery to a train: where is it going and where from? What does it carry and for what purpose? What places has it seen and which are left to see? And this: can I come along?

Something inside me wants to relinquish purpose, jump my personal track, hop this freight and wander, with it as my only guide.

The workers have paused with me to watch the train as it passed. I wonder if they feel as I do, that something came with that train, was here for only a moment and now has been carried off beyond reach. I wonder if they feel as I do now the train has gone - somehow, inexplicably a little more alone than before.

But they resume their labor, and I trek further along my unfinished road.

Tom Kiske

Truth and Knowledge

What is true of us? What is true of the world - the universe - in which we live?

Often, I think, the truth about such things is obscured by what we know of them. To borrow from the work of an anonymous 14th Century mystic, we face a "Cloud of Knowing" and it operates in two ways. First and simplest, what we think we know frequently turns out to be erroneous. At one point we knew the earth was flat and the center of the universe, everything revolving in perfect circles around us. Clearly, we did not know what we thought we knew.

In the second and perhaps more subtle sense, I believe it may be that the vast and steadily aggregating body of intellectual, rational, scientific and encyclopedic knowledge we've accumulated about the workings of the human mind and body, nature and the cosmos - even when completely factual and error-free - distracts us from an immediate "tactile" apprehension of ourselves and our surroundings both near and far. We have removed ourselves from the direct knowledge of things - the kind of intimate knowledge that a child has and which our primitive ancestors might once have possessed.

This is not to suggest that there's anything wrong with the pursuit of reasoned, explanatory knowledge, but rather that there are other equally valid ways of knowing. An in-depth, scientific treatise on pistils and stamens conveys no understanding of the feel of a rose petal, nor why the sight, smell and touch of the flower registers and resonates with something deep within. A lifetime studying musical form and notation, even if supplemented with a solid technical grasp of the principles and practice of audio engineering, will not explain the appeal of a certain symphony or Beatles tune, nor will it enable the scholar to compose a pleasing rondo or rhapsody.

And it worries me that in some future millennium, when we at last fully and factually know our world and know ourselves, we will discover that we have irretrievably lost both.

Small Spaces

It's small spaces that draw me,
Hidden places,
Caves,
Nooks, hollows,
Ancient almost buried ruins
And secret hideouts.

Darkness draws me
To the depths
And mysteries.

Cathedrals hold no interest,
Nor churches raising
Lofty spires
To the heavens.

Choirs sing angel harmonies,
But I believe He's
Resting in some
Small and quiet place,
Some long-forgotten chapel-burrow
Unconsecrated and unnamed,
Holy as the Earth.

So, yes, I like small spaces
Small and sacred
As a silent prayer.

How Tom Became Vice-President of the Science Fair

Back in 1960-61 the Greater St. Louis Science Fair was somewhat of a big deal. Kids from all over the area entered exhibits, and this was long before you could go to any grocery store and buy a kit with the 3-part cardboard backdrop now common for such exhibits. In those days it was all DIY, which resulted in some odd-looking setups, a few of which invariably collapsed or, worse, blew up.

Science - anything vaguely sciency - was huge, though. The Russkies were way ahead of us in a space race America didn't even know it was in until Sputnik announced to the world that we were second in a two-nation competition. Suddenly America went science crazy and the Science Fair assumed gargantuan importance. In such an environment, how did Tom, from a small inner city high school, ascend to the 2nd highest position in this program?

Well, some 60 years later Tom had all but forgotten the whole story until rummaging thru some of his mother's mementoes he came across a Post-Dispatch article featuring his election to high office. Then Tom's elderly but still mostly functional mind gradually reassembled the affair.

Every high school in the St. Louis area sent a delegate to the organization that put the event together. McKinley, for reasons lost to time, sent Tom. Here's the scene: 30 or more kids milling around in some hotel meeting room. Nobody quite understands why they're there or what they're supposed to do until some guy comes in and announces their first (and, we soon learned, *only*) job was to elect two officers, a president and a vice-president.

One kid jumped on this opportunity to achieve stardom. Robert was a short, dumpy-looking guy whose appearance suggested a future career as a banker, insurance agent or some obscure government bureaucrat. Robert (not Bob) immediately began aggressively working the room, buttonholing each clueless delegate in turn. "Hi, I'm Robert and I really, *really* want to be president." He's the only one who seems to care one way or the other, so it's not a tough sell.

Meanwhile, there's Tom, not a hint of an inkling of a notion about any Science Fair office. Instead, as usual, he's quietly just joking around with whoever's in the vicinity, his characteristic iconoclasm and sarcasm in clear contrast to the serious aspirations of Mr. R. I imagine it going something like this:

"I'd like to say a few words about Robert," Tom says.

After a minute or so of silence someone says, "Well, go on then."

"No, that was it," Tom says, "Those *were* the few words." Some titter, others just roll their eyes.

Finally, it's time to vote. Everyone writes their choice for president on a slip of paper, hands it in to the old guy in charge. Votes are tallied and to no-one's surprise, the future banker is elected to the top spot. He even got Tom's vote because, well, why not? Then the person getting the next-highest number of votes is announced as vice-president. Nobody is more astonished than Tom when he hears his name announced.

What? How the heck did that happen?

Only now, many years later, does Tom have a clue about this mystery. As he reflects on the demographics of the delegates, he recalls that a great majority of them were girls. So, he figures either:

A) female rivalry precluded many girls from voting for another girl, or

B) R's aggressive vote-soliciting pissed off almost as many delegates as it impressed, so they turned to the polar opposite, or

C) Tom was taller than almost all the delegates, humanoid and not wholly grotesque in appearance, so as they looked around the room the delegates saw . . . Tom. Or at least his head.

People have cast ballots in national elections based on criteria less well thought-out.

Regardless of how it happened, it turned out the responsibilities of the vice-president of the Greater St. Louis Science Fair were a lot like those of the Vice-President of the United States, meaning there weren't any. To this day Tom still takes immense pride in the fact that he handled this lack of responsibility in exemplary fashion.

What became of Robert? Who knows, but wherever folks are assembled to elect officers of some organization, I picture Robert skittering around imploring them to elect him president, because he really, *really* wants it. God bless him, and God save the United States of America.

Old St. Louis

The worn brick and cobblestone
Streets of my youth,
Are they haunted or am I?
I walk them nightly
When sleep eludes.
I hear the bells toll and threnody,
St. Agnes, St. Joe, Sts Peter and Paul.

I do not walk alone.
My ancestors, my boyhood friends,
Though passed, are there
To wave a greeting,
Sometimes accompany me a while,
Speaking a tongue the living cannot
know,
Then become mist and filament
And drift away
Like the scent of hops from the
breweries,
Yesterdays I cannot hold
Nor escape.

For though I am long gone from old
St. Louis,
St. Louis will never be gone from me.

The Superpowers of Aging

It is not widely known, but when we reach a certain advanced age new superpowers sometimes emerge. For example, I now possess a remarkable, almost uncanny power of forgetfulness. Why, just this morning I used it not once, but twice. First, leaving the pharmacy I forgot I'd planned to stop next at the bank directly across the street. Then, in the parking lot at Panera I walked away from my car forgetting the reading glasses I'd only moments before placed in a prominent position on the dash so as not to forget them. There are more dramatic examples, of course, but a fellow has to maintain *some* dignity.

Because it's an emerging superpower, it's yet to be fully developed. I did recover quickly from both my morning forgettings, but I'm confident I can hone this skill with time and practice. Once I perfect it, superforgetting is sure to come in handy. Like most of us, I have a number of unpleasant memories. How nice it will be once I can banish them to the land of the lost.

Heck, maybe I can use this superpower to make a buck. Got something you'd rather forget? Just tell me about it - presto, it's gone!

'Course I'll have to take care I don't inadvertently forget I have this superpower.

The Walls of Age

In the 17th Century John Donne wrote "any man's death diminishes me," emphasizing his connection to all mankind. It's a noble thought, but the truth is far more personal.

When you reach a certain age, you begin to feel the world closing in around you. It's as though time has been silently but inexorably erecting walls around you, walls that gradually isolate you from your own life, walls that are impenetrable and will never be breached. The mechanism by which this happens is subtle and invisible at first, but one day you wake up and there they are, surrounding you.

The loss of every relative or friend severs us from our own past, from the part of our life we shared with that person. No longer am I able to call my father and ask the name of the tune he whistled as we walked together the streets of the city when I was a boy. No more can my mother remind how my uncle took me for my first haircut, infuriating her. Walls are going up.

It doesn't hit you right away when you attend a boyhood friend's funeral, but maybe weeks or months later you'll think of calling to share a laugh over some goofy episode from your childhood. It's then you know that laugh is on the other side of a wall, never again to be shared, never again to be heard. You can't call Bryan, recite the first part of a line from a movie or show or comic book you saw together and have him immediately complete it with a chuckle. The same with Mitch and Mike and too many others. No more pickup basketball games and playful banter. So many carefree moments forever foreclosed, shut away, now confined to the land on the other side of the wall, a land you will never visit.

Perhaps worse, you don't forget those moments. They aren't erased. They don't disappear. If anything, they seem to grow and to glow. But it's a dim and wistful glow. What once brought laughter now summons only a sad smile. This walled-in cloister can seem ever lonelier and barren.

Walls behind you, but also ahead. The future which once stretched before you endlessly, ripe with promise and potential, now reaches only so far before it runs into the wall of your own mortality. The things you were going to do someday are just debris at the base of a wall marked Not Enough Time. It's as if you're living in 1970's Berlin but with no hope the walls might be torn down.

The sun still comes up every morning, though, and in its light other truths are revealed. If the past is foreclosed and the future foreshortened, that's not where you live anyway. Those walls can sharpen your perspective, your awareness of and appreciation for the present. It's not a bad place, the present. This is where the woman you love lives, where your children and grandkids live. If you've lost friends and relatives, others remain. The present is where the priceless gift of loving and being loved takes place. It's not behind any wall, it's right here, all around. Maybe the walls can teach us something: to *be* Present; to cherish all who are part of our lives today, right now, in this moment.

Perhaps that's lesson enough.

The Infamous Crestwood Plan

After two years of searching, we'd found our first home in the prosperous St. Louis suburb of Crestwood. It was far nicer than anything we'd seen; nicer than anything we expected. It had a huge backyard that joined all the others on the west side of Fox Creek Court as well as those behind us on Rayburn Road. There were no fences, just green lawns shaded by an extensive copse of tall, old-growth oaks whose canopies functioned as an arboreal squirrel highway. We were one house from the end of the cul-de-sac, beyond which the undeveloped Rayburn Park complemented our linked backyards, through which neighborhood children ranged freely, loosely watched over by us and the neighbors with whom we'd quickly made friends. Our children both learned to ride their bikes on Fox Creek Court, safe from the traffic on a more travelled street. It was in many ways an idyllic way of life.

Until.

A serious-looking woman came to our door one Saturday morning in 1969. "Are you aware of what's being planned for Crestwood?" she asked.

Uh-oh.

We invited her in, and after introducing herself as Norma Jean McC----, she went on to tell us the city had hired a consulting firm to develop a comprehensive plan for Crestwood's future. That actually sounded reasonable until Norma Jean explained that as part of the Plan, our tranquil cul-de-sac would be opened up, cutting through Rayburn Park and basically serving the businesses along Highway 66, which paralleled Fox Creek Court just beyond the homes across the street from us. More traffic. A lot more traffic. Not good. We were incensed!

"What can we do?" we asked.

"Well," she replied, "Would you be willing to help spread the word about this?"

And so we were recruited into an ad hoc group of "concerned citizens" setting out to foil the evil plot to wreck our neighborhood, disturb domestic tranquility and endanger our kids.

We obtained a copy of the Harland Bartholomew & Associates Comprehensive Plan Final Report and quickly learned it wasn't just Fox Creek Court that would be dramatically changed if the Plan were adopted, it was virtually all of Crestwood. The consultants had projected that traffic on Highway 66, already a busy highway bisecting Crestwood (and the nation), would rapidly grow to become a major bottleneck, impeding access to commercial interests and making it difficult for citizens to move freely around town. To prevent this, HBA proposed building a spider-like network of alternatives to 66. The downside, which they failed to mention, is that these alternate routes would draw heavy traffic into residential neighborhoods across the city.

What the city failed to realize is that the population of Crestwood was comprised of two demographics: retirees and young families. Older folks are notoriously hostile to change. The parents of those young families were men & women like P and me who'd come of age in the turmoil of the Sixties, and were already riled up about the steadily mounting number of American casualties in that little country in Southeast Asia. We weren't about to put up with any Crestwood horseshit!

We spread the word and as more and more people learned how their neighborhoods would be impacted by the HBA Plan, a small army of the Aroused and Indignant grew up around Paula & me, Norma jean and her husband, Jerry, and a handful of others. Meetings were held at our house and elsewhere which because of our age were serious but leavened with enough alcohol to also be fun parties. Through it, we strategized, drafted anti-Plan petitions and circulated them through a network of volunteers who went door-to-door gathering signatures.

D-Day was when city council met to consider adopting the HBA plan.

It was an early evening meeting July 8, 1969. Our nucleus group arrived early to ensure getting good seats. By the time the meeting was scheduled to begin, council chambers was packed! It was standing room only, folks lined 2 and 3 deep at the back and along both side walls. I'd come prepared with a speech but was astonished at the turnout, maybe even a bit intimidated, especially when I noticed the local press was covering the event.

As things got underway, several people rose to speak. Then it was my turn.

"Mayor Koenig and council members," I began, "Thank you for giving me this opportunity to speak. I represent a group of Crestwood citizens concerned and dismayed with the effect the HBA Comprehensive Plan will have upon our community."

I looked around the room, then continued, "From the size of the crowd present tonight, it would seem that a lot of people are similarly concerned – and dismayed. The fact that so many people are in attendance at this meeting is doubly surprising when you consider the conspicuous absence of publicity given the Comprehensive Plan."

I went on, detailing the many objections we had to the document, including the fact that nowhere did it state what the objective was. "A long-range comprehensive plan for a community should be designed to improve the quality of life of the residents of that community," I suggested, contrasting that with the way the Plan seemed instead to prioritize commercial and industrial expansion.

I gained confidence as I continued, "Now, if it is the will of the community that Crestwood become a commercial/industrial Mecca, then let the council adopt this plan." I paused & held up our petition with its hundreds of signatures. "But it's not what I want, it's not what the people whose names are on this petition want, and I don't think it's what any of the people around me want."

I looked around the room. "Is it?" I asked.

A resounding, full-throated roar of "NO!" from the crowd shook the rafters, punctuating my speech as I sat down.

The mayor and council members mumbled, harrumphed and quibbled among themselves, then voted unanimously to reject the Infamous Crestwood Plan. Really, what else could they do, confronted by constituents who seemed ready to transform instantaneously into a mob of villagers armed with pitchforks and torches?

Needless to say, the Kiske's hosted a celebratory afterparty and victory dance!

On a May Day only two years later, 40,000 or more Americans gathered in Washington, DC to protest the war in Vietnam. Although our sympathies were with them, we swear we were not responsible for that particular protest, nor were we swept up in the arrest of 12,000 protesters that followed – still today the largest mass arrest in US history.

There were three unexpected consequences of our efforts at mobilizing the community, two of which I'll divulge. First, to our great bemusement and amusement, for several years afterward, every Crestwood mayoral candidate felt they had to visit us hat in hand to win our endorsement. We'd apparently become "important people." At least within the modest perimeter of our suburban enclave.

Secondly, 40 years later and 750 miles distant, Paula & I would find ourselves called upon to reprise our role as rabble-rouse . . ., uh, that is, *community organizers.* In the second iteration, in our new home of College Station, our tranquil residential street was threatened not by the city but by a powerful developer with a plan that while not "comprehensive," was no less nefarious than HBA's. Fortunately, together with a handful of concerned neighbors, we were again able to mobilize the community and stymie the heinous designs of the Dark Side.

Mess with us at your peril, evildoers, The Force is strong with us!

Where Magic Lay

Magic there is to be found in woods and wells, caves and springs and old hollow trees where dwell the Old Ones, the Quiet Folk. Many lands have tales of such like, though none more than the Emerald Isle, home of the Tuatha De' Danann.

But is there not another favored habitat for the Little People and the spells they bring? Surely spirits of a certain breed must love places books are kept, libraries and book stores. Perhaps this is where many of the Faerie have fled, weakened and disheartened by modern man's indifference.

Seldom have I visited a bookstore and not come away bearing the talisman of some strange enchantment, hastened home with it anxious to open its cover and be drawn within, there to live for a day or a week, far from here, far from now, in a curious landscape amidst new-found friends and unheard-of creatures.

For magic, though, a library is best. A borrowed book is dusted not only with Faerie magic, but also carries the lingering touch of all who visited there before, took something from its words and phrases, but left a subtle trace of themselves behind. Here a human mind has foraged, perhaps found nourishment.

As I've not encountered a name for these book spirits, it falls to me to provide them identity. Comes to me now, this: The Librii. Dusky, dusty folk, they, ancient and knotted as all wisdom, yet spry and sprightly as a new idea, in whose light they iridesce, become brilliantly beautiful. All Librii wear glasses, though whether they need them or not isn't known. Shy and soft-spoken creatures are these and only open minds hear their beckoning whisper. At times they are virtually invisible and their presence can be detected only in the form of a musty aroma, coupled with a barely audible crackling sound like old, yellowed pages crumbling.

Above all else The Librii value freedom, honesty and respect. Woe be the man who seeks to restrain a Libris, or speak ill or falsely of one, for he will be doomed to a dumb, dull life forever after, locked away in a cold, dark chamber where no light shines, no music plays, no warmth ever comes.

Unlike most Little People, the Librii are unimpressed with gifts of food or drink. Instead, leave them but a brief note written in your own hand – a thought well expressed, a feeling well described, a story well told – and The Librii will offer you uncommon gifts, gleaming treasures nowhere else to be found.

Librii share with most Faerie an aversion to iron and electricity in all forms. Their ways are old ways and they are slow to change. They may find barns noble, crannies ok, but they are not neighborly to Nooks nor kind to Kindles.

Our Artificial Lives

Good morning, everyone and welcome to the seminar. This morning I'll be speaking with you about the artificiality of life in the 21ˢᵗ Century. Please hold your questions until the end. Likewise, your catcalls, curses, boos, hoots and vegetable-tossing.

So, what do I mean by the artificiality of life?

The concept is a simple one but the incidence of the phenomenon is pervasive. Most of us today are city dwellers. Most of us work inside - in an office, a factory or warehouse, or a retail establishment of some kind. Traveling to and from work we're typically inside some mechanical conveyance - a car, a bus, a train. If we walk at all it is normally on a paved surface, often with one or both eyes focused on a "smart" phone & sometimes with both ears covered by a headset drowning out ambient sounds while injecting electronic music directly inside our skulls.

Home is obviously inside and our entertainment together with much of what we know about the day's events comes to us by way of pixels on an ever-shifting screen. Even our currency & wealth exists in the form of a small plastic rectangle or electronic bits and bytes stored on some distant computer. Maybe in an imaginary "cloud."

Consider even something as basic as the food we take into our bodies. Most of what we eat is "processed" - a chemical concoction engineered for shelf life or to ensure that we crave more and more, a recipe for obesity, diabetes and a host of other ills. Nutritional value - who cares? You want fries with that?

There's even an emerging second-order artificiality. We can now double down on our artificial lives by donning a pair of goggles that separate us completely from the environment and fully submerge us into a realm that's wholly electronic.

None of this is real in the sense that a tree or a river is real. None of it is natural. It's artificial, artifice, artifact. We are surrounded by and immersed in things that do not grow of themselves, but things that are made, manufactured. Most of what we see and hear, most of what we interact with is a product, the embodiment of human commerce.

Doubtless, such things have made our lives easier, more comfortable. But have they distorted our view of reality; of the real world we inhabit but to which we seldom attend? Has the artificial environment blinded us to the larger world, the greater universe outside the snug plastic cocoon we've erected around ourselves? Have we become the "tired, nerve-shaken, over-civilized people" about which John Muir long ago warned?

We'll examine such questions further in our next lecture.

Hey - where'd everyone go??!!

Tom Kiske

Will There Be Room?

How different it is for we who've become disillusioned with what is called progress, who are not concerned with attracting new business to our community, who do not view the prospect of a road-widening or a new shopping center with unalloyed joy.

Are you one of us? Are you troubled by the idea of a future world that is one immense city, paved and crowded with our kind living so close together we must draw in our shoulders as we do today on airliners? Do you worry a time may come when we will drink not water but chemicals, breathe not air but fumes? Are you disturbed by the likely fate of the bluebird, the prairie dog, the butterfly, when their habitat is only concrete and steel?

Do you sometimes ask yourself - when the woods and wildlife are gone, when the small spaces are all crushed by bulldozers preparing a path for the high-rise or landfill, when the free-flowing creeks and streams are all straightened to channelized ditches or buried in concrete - will there be room for me?

If your thoughts wander this way even only occasionally, then like Thoreau you are out of step with your fellows.

And there is hope.

Time and Age

Time is a subject that's long intrigued me – and others. Ancient Greeks split time in two: Chronos was the god of chronological time, the kind measurable today in minutes, hours and days; Kairos, his brother, ruled over a different sort of time, unmeasurable except broadly, in terms of emotional or spiritual impact. It's the time of experiences, experiences where we "lose all sense of time," where we're "in the moment."

Children live in Kairos time, play time. You'd expect older folks – like me – might as well, retired, free from alarm clocks and deadlines. But it ain't necessarily so, as the Gershwin song goes. Although we may be somewhat less dominated by clocks and calendars, our Golden Years still demand a measure of obeisance to Chronos. We have appointments – for doctors and dentists, for appliance repairs, for hair cuts and "styling," for flights and a dozen other requirements pf today's way of life.

Then too, our time is constrained. There are days we just don't feel well, our ability to do what we want or what's expected of us is diminished by fatigue, injury, illness and age, as well as the responsibilities and duties of family and friendship.

We aren't free.

We know our End Time approaches ever nearer and cannot be avoided. Time will win, will ultimately defeat us. We know this, but must we face that inevitability as time's slaves?

At my age I stand imperiled on a narrow ledge above the bottomless abyss and my balance isn't so good. My legs tremble. I wobble and teeter. For God's sake, DON'T LOOK DOWN!"

Wouldn't you think our species would've been equipped with some kind of warning lights or maybe shrill buzzers or an Alexa-type voice saying. "Caution! Caution! Old age approaching!"? At the very least we should've come from the factory with an Owner's Manual. The last chapter might detail the signs of approaching decrepitude, maybe a few helpful hints about steps a person might take to ease the transition from vigor to rigor.

Oh, hell, nobody reads owner's manuals anyway. Besides, if we knew what was in store for us, drug companies couldn't possibly keep up with the demand for Valium and other pharmaceuticals. Still, I can't escape the feeling that either evolution of The Big Guy let us down.

On the other hand, at least a fellow's spirit can still be lifted by the sight of a girl in shorts, a miniskirt or tight-fitting jeans. Maybe it's not so bad.

I been busy. Busy with the usual concerns of daily living. Things break – refrigerators, for example – then you have taxes that demand your attention and about a million and a half little things like taking out the trash, doctor visits times two, grocery shopping, birthdays, Holidays and other such events. The list seems both trivial and endless. These things occupy your mind, trouble your sleep, and when you're not dealing with them or worrying about potential disasters on the horizon, you're seeking escape watching TV, reading, texting or emailing.

No wonder we all wander around dazed and exhausted. We have no time or energy left to attend to the needs of the human soul. It's as Thoreau warned: we risk looking back over our lives at the hour of our death and realizing we never truly lived.

Worse, we make this realization repeatedly, yet too soon it fades from our frantic minds and we revert to functioning as mere cogs in a vast machine without purpose save self-perpetuation. We're slaves to an unknown master, or perhaps to a master we only assume exists, but doesn't. It's just the machine.

What's the answer? I know not, but neither have I abandoned the search.

From the Journal of Tom

I've kept a Journal since October, 1962. I was 19, attending Washington University. On the first page of Volume I, I wrote "This is the very personal account of every thought and emotion I entertain written as soon as possible after experiencing it. The purpose of the narration is two-fold. First, it provides me an outlet for bottled-up thoughts. Second, in the future, this Journal may be the key to success either (hopefully) directly or indirectly."

On the last page of Volume I, this appears: "... ever feel like nobody? Well, I did ... and do. I don't know what to say except I feel my life is hanging in the balance right now and that, depending on a few decisions, I will either be a very cool person or go completely down the drain. And making no decision is a decision in itself."

It was not a happy time for Tom.

Sixty years and sixty Volumes later, the Journal's still going, despite a hiatus of a decade or so in the 1970's. The tenor of the writing has grown less dark and the purpose of the Journal has evolved. Here are a few excerpts from Volume LX (August, 2020 – August, 2023).

Page 69:

"In the Journal I'm having a conversation with myself. The Journal is a quest for understanding – making sense of myself, the world around me and the things that happen. With understanding – or maybe even just with the search for it – comes a certain internal peace. In this way, sitting at a small table with a cup of coffee, letting thoughts rumble thru my consciousness and flow out into these pages is a form of meditation, of contemplation.

Perhaps I'm alone in this, but the daily input from my senses doesn't automatically sift and sort itself. Lacking articulation, it doesn't self-organize. I have to write about it or the lessons life tries to teach are lost.

And there are so many lessons, so much to learn while we draw breath and walk upon the Earth."

Page 15:

"The last page of The Atlantic is always an ode. The current issue (Sept.) is entitled 'Not Being a Morning Person.' It's more an essay than an ode, and although not destined for The Best Essays of 2021, it includes a creative characterization of the way I feel upon awakening.

'...it's arduous; it's real. Deflector shields gone. Resilience: none. The world is upon you ... a ghastly payload of noise and glare and babbling, galumphing people. You'll be okay, you'll get there, but you need time. Complex operations of personal reassembly are required... every morning ... you build yourself anew.'

The author, a staff writer at The Atlantic, is James Parker – and he knows whereof he writes. I cannot claim status as a morning person or non-morning person, but it does take a while for me to reassemble myself in the morning. It takes longer for my son to do so and he more clearly falls into the 'not' category.

It seems to me one's morning orientation changes with age. I am definitely more morning at 77 ¾ than I was at 18 or 25. I think, tho, that the requirement for reassembly is more a function of where one falls on the introvert/extrovert scale. More introvert ' more reassembly.

Some days, too, that complex process goes somewhat awry. A few parts are missing or left over. The final product isn't a finished product. the thrusters are misaligned, some sensors are connected wrong or the stabilizers are out of balance. Maybe you make it thru the day, but your performance is sub-par; you feel 'off' or weird.

Try again tomorrow. Get your act together, because just maybe, after all, it's just a

Page 21:

"Thursday, February 16, 2021
........Breaking News.......................Breaking News.............

TOM FEELS SHITTY TODAY

ap.CSTX

Informed sources highly places within the Kiske household have said that the normally ebullient Mr. Kiske is 'just not himself today.' They went on to reveal that this isn't the first time the Head of Household has suffered a difficult 24 hours. Altho these sources indicated sympathy for Mr. Kiske's condition, nonetheless they did call in question his ability to discharge his responsibilities , chief among them keeping everyone entertained.

Meanwhile, Mr. Kiske's Chief of Staff and Press Secretary (Mr. Kiske) dismissed these claims as 'Pure Bullshit' and suggested they're just more evidence of a vast right-wing conspiracy. 'Hell,' said Kiske, 'I done the Jumble jest fine this morning!'

For more on this, go to our website, fecesbook page, or just make something up and spread it around.

In other news, everything everywhere sucks!"

When Normal Slips Away

"Life is a constant battle to maintain order in a Universe that runs to disorder."
Erwin Schrodinger

There's much to be said for mere normality. After a crisis has passed, breathing comes easier, the shine is restored to things, all instruments are in tune and harmony is at least possible.

We live close to the edge. All of us. For the most part, we choose to ignore how precarious our perch, how uncertain our footing, how slippery our grasp on the things we treasure. The landscape ahead seems level, firm, inviting. It stretches to a far horizon too distant for our vision, too many miles and hours away to warrant worry or care.

But then a deep rumbling passes underfoot, trees and mountains sway, man-made monuments tumble down and great fissures open in the fundament all around. Stability and constancy were illusions. There is no fixed point for reckoning in this strange, shifting terrain. We falter, stumble, fall.

Everything we knew, all that we relied on is wiped away and the icy fingers of fear wrap 'round our hearts. The unknown is upon us.

It is in such times our gaze must turn upward and there in the vast blue heavens, in the eternal grace that remains when everything else is lost - it is there we must find our hope, our courage and the pole star by which we can navigate thru the darkness to the promise of tomorrow and tomorrow and tomorrow.

This trembling, troubled world doesn't matter. This is not our home.

The Ape in the Attic

When I was a boy, my mother would sometimes take me out to my cousin's house for a visit. As we did not have a car at the time, the trip from inner city St. Louis to the suburb of Webster Groves meant a long ride involving multiple transfers among a number of buses and trolleys. To me it was a fine adventure, with the promise of more adventures to come because my mom would leave me there for a few days so I could play with my cousin Tommy.

I had plenty of friends at home to play with, so I think the real idea was for me to get to know my cousins: Tommy, who was two years my junior, and Peggy, six months older than me. I always looked forward to these visits as Tommy was as eager for mischief as me and Peggy was a pretty girl and although she was my cousin and thus technically off-limits for hanky-panky, limits are for testing, aren't they?

Now I have to confess that the events of this tale might have taken place over the course of more than one visit. I sure hope they did because some parts demand a level of stupidity which might be forgiven an 11-year-old but would be inexcusable at 13. I'm going to begin with 13-year-old me.

Invasion #1

Our first day together, Tommy and I filled with so much adventure and mischief (which is best left undocumented) that by evening we'd run out of things to do. Fortunately, a scary movie was playing at a theater within walking distance, so after dinner off we went.

The film was the original version of "Invasion of the Body Snatchers," starring Dana Wynter (Whoa – hot stuff!) and Kevin McCarthy, who was so cool I decided to add "Kevin" to my name, becoming Thomas H. Kevin Kiske. Some old friends still believe that to be my full name.

Anyway, it was a good movie and suitably scary, so we decided to watch it again the next night. This time, however, Peggy came along, as did Carolyn, who was their neighbor, Tommy's age and kinda cute in a pre-teen, coltish way. To the casual observer, this could've been mistaken for a double-date, but it was just a group of cousins and friends going to the movies. Or so it began.

Somehow, Peggy and I found ourselves sitting together, which meant so did Tommy and Carolyn. In those days, at 13 I was very shy and woefully ignorant and inexperienced when it came to the opposite sex, plus there was the whole girl-cousin taboo, so no hand-holding going on there.

In retrospect, I think it's possible Peggy was a little disappointed in that, albeit equally uncertain how to navigate the cousin thing. Her approach was this: during the scary parts of the movie, she'd turn away from the screen towards me, grab my arm and start scratching. "Let me scratch you!" she said.

What?

Now I was truly baffled. Is this normal, I wondered. I didn't say anything in response, which she evidently took as assent or at least acquiescence, so I got seriously scratched a half dozen or more times as bodies were being snatched and the snatchers chased lovely Dana and handsome Kevin hither and yon. By the end of the movie, my right arm looked like it had been mauled by a mountain lion.

Yes, it was a little painful but it was okay. I'd sat next to a girl - even if she was my cousin - in a darkened movie theater and there was some touching involved – even if it was just her fingernails leaving angry red marks up and down my arm.

After the movie, we all walked home together without further touching or scratching, but the new, "Kevin" version of me felt he'd made a small step forward. No, I hadn't gotten to first base; hell, I hadn't even come up to bat, but maybe at least I'd gotten out of the dugout. For sure I was on my way being a full-fledged teenager and a real cool dude.

Invasion #2

In this part, I'm younger; maybe eleven. My "Pre-Kevin" days. At least I hope I am.

My cousins lived in a big, old sprawling house. Tommy and Peggy each had their own rooms, whereas at home I slept on a hide-a-bed sofa in the front of a 3-room "flat." The best part of my cousins' house, though, was that it had an attic. A full-size attic running the length of the house, tall enough to walk in upright. And it was full of stuff.

All kinds of stuff. Furniture, trunks, mirrors, sporting goods, lamps, boots and shoes, tons of stuff in boxes large and small, all covered in dust. It was stuff in limbo, no longer meriting a place in the living area of the house, but clinging to enough value that it couldn't be just put out in the trash.

It was an ideal place for kids to root around in. If that were permitted, which it wasn't in my cousins' house.

Still, one afternoon Tommy and I found ourselves alone in the house, a situation in which the normal rules begged to be transgressed. "Wanna go up in the attic?" Tommy asked.

"Let's go!"

He opened the door and began climbing the stairs into the attic. Only a few steps up, Tommy screamed, leaped down, slammed the door and ran lickety-split down the hall to his room as though being chased by the devil himself. When I finally caught up with him, he was still shaking so bad he couldn't speak.

At length he calmed down enough to answer when I asked what was wrong.

"There's a gorilla in the attic!" he exclaimed.

This sounded dumb even for my cousin, who once thought that federal prison in San Francisco Bay had been named for Chicago's notorious gangster. You know, Al Capone.

"A gorilla?" I said, incredulously.

"Yeah," Tommy said, "He was hanging over the banister at the top of the stairs."

"How the heck would a gorilla get in your attic?" I scoffed.

"I don't know, but he's up there." Tommy wasn't joking, wasn't trying to prank me. He was genuinely scared.

Now a year or two earlier, I'd read a lot of Edgar Allan Poe, including "Murders in the Rue Morgue", so I was aware that gorillas have a proclivity for showing up in unlikely places and perpetrating dastardly deeds, even - murder! Still, in my cousin's attic? Unlikely.

I strode confidently and bravely back down the hall. Easing the attic door open, I climbed the first step, looked up, and there was the damn gorilla hanging over the banister, reaching down for me with both hairy arms!

Back in Tommy's room a split second later I said, "There's a gorilla in your attic, man!"

"Told ya," he said.

My immediate thought was to call the cops. They'd know how to handle this. Heck, maybe they were already dealing with a simian crime wave, probably keeping it quiet to avoid a public panic.

"No," Tommy said, "No cops. Not yet."

So, instead of summoning the Webster Groves police or even Animal Control, we walked up the street to a gas station where Tommy "knew a guy" who'd help us.

Turns out the "guy" was a kid who pumped gas. He was only a few years older than us. Enough older, though, that he scoffed at the notion of a gorilla in the attic.

"You kids are nuts," he pronounced.

Still, we persisted, gradually wearing him down, 'til he grudgingly agreed to come along and debunk the ape in the attic story. Yeah, he didn't believe us but he still picked up a baseball bat standing at my cousin's door - just in case he might have to conk a gorilla or something.

The three of us climbed up to the second floor and down the hall to the attic door, my cousin and me huddled behind the bigger kid. He eased the door open, went up that first step and looked up, just like I'd done earlier. He flinched, jerked back, but he didn't run. Instead, he took a longer look upward. Then he started laughing.

"Come here, you little jerks," he chuckled.

We did as he asked, albeit a bit timorously. By now the big kid was halfway up the attic steps. We watched in awe as he grabbed hold of one of the ape's arms and started waving it at us.

What the ...?

Only then did we realize that the ape in the attic was my aunt's fur coat, its arms dangling over the banister.

Probably a good thing we hadn't called the cops.

Unfilled, Unhurried

Time.

Unfilled time. Perhaps the most precious resource available. Unfilled time is not vacant time, not empty time, not time to be "killed."

It's unhurried time, unburdened time. It's time that is solely your own. It does not belong to others. It is not chained to awaiting tasks, not clouded by worry, not narrowed and blindered by needed focus.

It's free, and it frees your mind and your spirit; maybe your soul. It releases those gentler aspects of yourself from the constricting tethers of duty, responsibility and goal-seeking. The best parts of you, parts that the racket and rumble of daily demands shoves aside and crams into a cramped, dark corner - is released, expands to its true, unconstrained dimensions and shape, breathes deep, asserts its neglected presence and sings its subtle truth: this, not all that busy, frantic, crusty jumble, *this* is me!

Through the kitchen window I watch the dawn brighten the heavenward tips of the trees in the untamed woods beyond the fence. Slowly the morning sun spreads its soft light downward along Spring's fresh forest foliage, then dances nearer the table where I sit with my coffee. Something out there whispers to something in here, inside me - *This is where all that is real abides. Come and find it.*

Come.

𝔄 Dopey Poetry Contest

I do not recall where I learned of it, likely some internet thing. It was simple, literate and ultimately stupid. In other words, right up my alley! The idea was, take the first line from a well-known poem, then make up your own second line. Here are mine:

Shakespeare –
Shall I compare thee to a summer's day?
Hot for sure; too bad you're gay.

Robert Blake
Tyger, tyger, burning bright
Flaming tigers, what a sight!

Robert Burns
O my Love's like a red, red rose
'Specially her bright red nose

Wordsworth
I wandered lonely as a cloud
A fart can sure disperse a cloud

Brooke
If I should die, think only this of me
An electric fence is no place to pee

Edgar Allan Poe
Once upon a midnight dreary
I wrote a poem that's really sceery

I don't know if a contest winner was ever announced. Just a fun challenge, really.

The Snidge

Watch out for The Snidge when comes this December
It's something that really you ought to remember

A Snidge may be hiding there under a bridge
Or lurking by something inside of your fridge

Now that Christmas is coming so close and so near
You do NOT want a Snidge anywhere around here

For The Snidge, he's a rascal, he'll create such a fuss
'Cuz The Snidge, as we know, he's just not like us

You and I, we're always so shiny and sunny
But The Snidge, oh my gosh, he looks kind of funny

His head is too big, or maybe too small
No, his parts just don't fit together at all

Some Snidges are green and others are blue
They're not the same color as me or as you

Snidge noses are too long & their necks are too short
And once, in a church a Snidge let a fart

To do that in church is some kind of sin
Tthat's why some churches won't let a Snidge in

Yes, a Snidge's behavior is often outrageous
And some, I've been told, are highly contagious

Tom Kiske

Folks like us, to be sure, are invariably nice
While Snidges, we know, carry bedbugs and lice

And Snidges, last night I heard on the news
Why, some of them harbor unusual views

We do not know in truth just how a Snidge thinks
But we're all pretty sure that every Snidge stinks

I've not yet met a Snidge, this much it is true
But I know deep inside they're not like me and you

You and I are alike and for that we are glad
For you know to be different's just got to be bad

Oh, Love Your Neighbor's a rule we maybe should try
But to Snidges I'm certain it doesn't apply

For if you talk to a Snidge you may find in the end
Oh my gosh and my golly, you've a Snidge for a friend

And though your Snidge friend may not try to hurt ya
Other friends you once had soon may desert ya

Alas, when toward others we don't act as we ought
We may have forgotten the lessons He taught

To learn them anew, here's a good way to start
It's not how you look, it's what's in your heart.

So Snidges, you see, are not bad at all
Merry Christmas to Snidges, Merry Christmas to all.

Two Friends, or A Letter to Mitch

April 29, 2003

Dear Mitch -

I'm writing this at Methodist Hospital here in Houston, where I'm continuing my battle versus The Big C, as you are there in St. Louis. I'm here for the "ultra-sensitive" PSA I have done every six weeks or so. It's been percolating upward and once it hits the Magic Number of 1.0, I'll be going into a clinical trial of some experimental drugs to keep this damn thing at bay - I hope.

As you may know, I've written a couple of little articles for McKinleygoldbugs.com and the guy who put the website together has been after me to do more. Over the weekend I'd come up with an idea for another piece - basically about jobs we had while in HS, and thinking back, it occurred to me that pretty much every job I had, you and I had together. From stacking stools in the cafeteria before school to the infamous Sunshine Laundry to Fouke Fur to Sverdrup, seems like we almost always did things together. I remember going to get our work permits together, and of course, our social security cards.

I'm sure there are a lot of guys across the country who consider themselves really good friends, but I'd be willing to bet you could count on the fingers of one hand, those who actually know each other's social security number. That has to be pretty damn special, buddy.

There has to be a measure of irony in the fact that now, so many years down the road, we're both going thru this cancer bullshit together, too. Who would have thought, when we were enjoying a nice baloney sandwich lunch at your house before going back to haul rugs at Sunshine, that forty years later we'd be having THIS kind of baloney together?

I don't know about you, but for me the worst part of this cancer crap (*well, aside from going around for several weeks with a tube sticking out of my censored*) is - I can't figure out who to sue. I mean, there's gotta be <u>somebody</u>. It was probably asbestos at Sunshine, but hell, that company is long gone. Maybe Miss Boese is still around, the teacher who lined us up with that job. Maybe we can sue her. Yeah, that's the ticket. Punitive damages. Shouldn't be hard at all to find a sheister - ooops, I mean a lawyer - to take the case.

Of course, there are some things about cancer that aren't so bad (*aside from that tube in the censored*) - I mean, I don't worry a whole lot about my diet these days, and it seems maybe I get just a tad less nagging from the spouse. Actually, one of my prize moments was during the recovery from my surgery when Paula made the comment, "Geez, Tom, I didn't realize how much you did around here." YES! Now there's a marital moment to remember. Just wish I'd had a tape recorder.

But seriously, I think you learn something from this lousy disease. For me, it was learning to accept the care and affection of others. That may sound strange, but you might relate to it. Like most guys, I was all about taking care of business - protecting the wife and family, shielding them from harm or even, as much as possible, from being aware of the possibility bad things could happen. Then, all of a sudden you find yourself flat on your back and not *able* to take care of things anymore. It's a shock. You don't have a whole lot of choice but to lay back and let others handle things, including your own sorry ass. It's kind of humbling, but it's also an eye-opener, or at least it was for me.

Until "The C", I'd never really thought about the fact that there were people who genuinely cared about me - yes, who loved me. When that realization came home, it was one of the most powerful experiences I've ever had. And my life has not been the same since. It might be shorter than I thought it would be, but it's also a helluva lot sweeter. Every day and every hour seem more precious. I'm sure you know what I mean.

So, anyway, buddy, you hang in there and we'll battle this f*cker together. I know you're in good hands there with Madline taking care of you and making sure you don't get too wild and crazy. When things get rough, just remember, it could be worse - *you could have a tube sticking out of your censored.*

And you know what - they say visualization can help. Create a mental image of those cancer cells self-destructing. I visualize mine as teeny, tiny little exploding minions. Give it a try!

And remember there's a shitload of folks who care about you - who love you, Mitch - and one of them is me.

(Note: Mitch would die of metastatic colon cancer not long after this letter was mailed).

Tom Kiske

𝓐 𝓑reed 𝓐part

Great brown pelicans skim lazily over the murky waters of Galveston Bay, their smooth grace lifting us, the wingless watchers on the shore. The pelicans' season here is brief and reminds us ours is as well, we who seek our own form of grace. We who may have a Watcher of our own, waiting, perhaps, to see if angels' feathers or serpents' scales evolve. Wistful, maybe, for what we lack, something far beyond our ken

Even balmy climes have clouds.

So, the dark hours. The darkness. Breaker insinuates himself into the conversation. He has become so familiar to me that despite his umbrous visage, despite his grim beckoning, he seems almost a friend. Certainly a companion.

Then, I'm in St. Louis with my oldest, closest buddies. A brew or two. An hour, maybe more, of laughter, teasing, the happy and effortless persiflage in a shorthand open only to those with a fifty-year bond. So pleasant I want only to stay, to linger in this beautiful, playful warmth.

But he shows up. Unseen, but his presence makes itself felt until my eyes adapt, see beyond their usual limitations. There he stands, leaning against the wall, staring at me somber faced. I want to ignore him but cannot. He nods toward the door and although I do not wish to go, I am summoned away.

Outside.

Breaker never speaks but leaves me alone with myself and my cold, awful silence. I recognize that something is off, here, but I know not what. Some vital something is missing – maybe missing from me.

It may be that Breaker wears the backward collar, calls me to Confession. But it's years too late for that. I've forgotten more sins than I remember, nor have I ever found or earned that requisite state of grace.

So I walk alone, or maybe sit, and if I had the habit I'd surely smoke, while the fun slips away and the shadows gather.

Maybe after a while I'll go back inside. I'll cover up, wear a smile. But my smile will be attenuated, for I am on some further shore. I am a breed apart. I watch with the Watcher.

𝓟𝓪𝓻𝓽 𝓣𝔀𝓸

Some Opinions

Most of these appeared in *The Eagle*, the local newspaper for Bryan, College Station and Brazos County, Texas, circa 2020-2023.

Is Reconciliation Possible?

In the real world the election is over and Donald Trump lost. Just over half of Americans are smiling, the rest either frowning or snarling. Frowners, for the most part, have accepted defeat and moved on. In Snarlerworld, their guy won but a sinister conspiracy somehow stole his victory. Smilers' jubilation is tempered by the same troubling question Frowners are asking: how could so many folks vote for the other side?

It's clear that America remains more divided, often viciously so, than almost any time in history. What we all should be asking today is, are our differences irreconcilable, the rift separating us so wide and deep that our very union is threatened? Is the only solution a divorce far more complex and destructive than that attempted in 1860? Will history record that the American decline and fall was precipitated by our nation's political balkanization into a hodge-podge of little red units and blue units squabbling amongst themselves, each too weak to avoid conquest by hostile forces from afar?

A patriot would hope not, but what would it take to heal our wounds and bring us together as a nation with a diversity of views and opinions but Americans all, tolerant of those with whom we disagree? Arguably, five critical conditions must be met to prevent partisan rancor from pushing America to the breaking point.

First and perhaps most obviously, the two sides must both have the desire to reconcile. Each must realize that a continuing state of verbal warfare is not in their own interest, does not advance their cause and damages the fabric of democracy. Most of the population at large already recognize this. Too many party leaders, though, as yet do not.

What might bring the factions together and persuade them to subordinate their partisan agenda to a larger, more compelling common cause? For an example we might look to the Dayton Peace Accords, the 25th anniversary of which was recently celebrated. The Accords basically ended the long war among ethnic groups formerly subsumed within Yugoslavia. What finally brought the Serbs, Croats and Bosniaks together is simple: they got tired of killing each other. One would hope a quarter of a million Americans dead of the Covid-19 pandemic might suffice to bring Republican and Democratic leadership together. Thus far it has not.

Secondly, there must be sufficient common ground to provide a basis for ongoing cooperation, coupled with recognition that "compromise" is not a dirty word and that jockeying for position over who gets credit for progress or blame for mistakes is both unproductive and childish in the public eye. Especially today America has a burgeoning list of urgent needs acknowledged by both parties which can only be met by working together.

Thirdly, both sides must realize that extremes - be they left or right - are at best obstacles to what's realistically achievable and at worst turn otherwise sympathetic people against your cause. Calls to defund the police no doubt cost Democrats votes among Independents just as senseless chants of "Lock her up" did for Republicans. Moreover, Newton's Third Law of Motion - for every action there's an equal and opposite reaction - seems to apply to the political realm as well. Extremism on the right begets extremism on the left.

Fourth, everyone must be willing to tune out the fomenters - those who make a living from keeping folks riled up - be they radio or tv ranters or political opportunists. There must also be a commitment to stop vilifying the other side. Not all Trump supporters were wackadoodle racist Snarlers. Likewise, not all Democrats were Commies lusting for free stuff - which, by the way, I've yet to receive.

It would also be helpful to take a break from Facebook, Twitter and similar social media with their curated feeds that shelter users from the discomfort of views different from their own. Further, as we've learned, the internet has been co-opted as a 21st Century Trojan Horse, built not of wood but of malicious misinformation spread virally by sources foreign and domestic to sow confusion and discontent.

Finally, we must allow time for our wounds to begin healing, time to detox from the addictive adrenalin rush of the constant drumbeat summoning us to battle neighbors we're told are either America-haters or fascists bent on the destruction of our cherished way of life.

Meanwhile, if you listen closely, you may hear the echo of a John Lennon refrain from 1969. It's a growing chorus of Americans voicing in harmony their plea: "This-ism, that-ism, ism, ism, ism - all we are saying is give peace a chance."

Happy 2nd of July

Was there a President before Washington? Did we declare independence before The Declaration of Independence? Does it matter?

Some of the names are etched in our collective memory: Washington, Jefferson, Adams, Franklin, Paine, Hamilton, John Hancock. But there were 56 signatures on the Declaration of Independence including that of the improbably named Button Gwinnett. These were the men who came together to transform a disparate group of English colonies into what would become an independent nation. They knew that in signing that revolutionary document they risked everything, their possessions, their positions, their very lives. From an English perspective they were traitors and the penalty for treason was well known. They knew they had to remain steadfast and united. As Franklin told them, "We must all hang together, or most assuredly, we shall all hang separately." Signing was an act of astonishing courage and trust. They were facing the greatest army the world had ever seen. Victory was far from assured. The Declaration itself emerged only after a year of arguing, haggling and negotiation.

The Second Continental Congress convened in Philadelphia May 10, 1775, shortly after the battles of Lexington and Concord. Delegates had been chosen by each of the colonies, in some cases by maneuvers of dubious legality. Not all of them were authorized to vote for independence. Some were forbidden to do so. As the first order of business, they elected Virginia's Peyton Randolph as leader. Few today recognize his name, but his title was President, making Peyton arguably the first President of the United States. His term, however, was brief. He collapsed and died October 22, 1775 while dining with his cousin, Thomas Jefferson. He was succeeded by John Hancock, who took on the herculean task of achieving consensus among a loose assemblage of colonies with little in common but a sense of grievance with how King George was treating them.

Remarkably, the efforts of Hancock and a handful of other leaders, coupled with the intransigence and arrogance of George III and the British Parliament, the Continental Congress came to acknowledge that independence was the only way to end the growing political and economic abuse they were suffering under English rule. Only a year after the Congress convened, even colonies that had initially resisted severing ties with England agreed, authorizing Congress to adopt a resolution first proposed by Richard Henry Lee of Virginia entitled A Resolution for Independence. The much longer Declaration wasn't finalized until two days later, so shouldn't Independence Day more properly be July 2?

The larger question, though, is why did Congress feel it necessary to publish a Declaration of Independence? After all, we'd already been at war with England for more than a year and nobody thought reconciliation was possible.

The answer is in the first paragraph, ". . . a decent respect for the opinions of mankind" requires declaring the reasons for the separation. What an extraordinary message those words imply: we're doing this not just for ourselves, but for mankind. The authors of this document were writing in the liberating spirit of John Locke and The Enlightenment as they continued, "We hold these truths to be self-evident, that all men are created equal . . .." ALL men, not just Americans, have the right to life, liberty and the pursuit of happiness.

Obviously, from our 2023 perspective those truths were shamefully limited in scope. When they said men they specifically meant white males. Women? People of color? The Founders left those questions for future battles. We cannot fault them for failing to predict sensibilities a century or two in the future. What they accomplished with the Declaration was a gigantic step forward for humanity: conferring newfound dignity on common people and acknowledging that they, not just kings and noblemen, have certain rights simply by virtue of being born; rights no one can take from them.

While the Declaration goes on to fulfill its stated purpose of justifying separation by listing at least 27 specific instances of injury England has inflicted upon the American colonies, the radical idea that we are blessed from birth with fundamental and inalienable rights is what inspired people around the world in 1776, and continues to do so in 2023. That, as well as our nations' founding, is what we should celebrate amid the bbq and fireworks, affirming our commonality as Americans above our differences and like the Founders, pledging to each other our lives, our fortunes and our sacred honor. Not for a day, but every day.

𝓦ho's to 𝓑lame?

It's possible many of the woes that plague us today derive from an unexplored dimension of the human psyche. Call it blame-seeking. When times are unsettled and upsetting, when things go against us, when we feel powerless in the face of immense forces, when we seem to be playing against a stacked deck - we want someone to blame. We need someone to blame.

It's not a new phenomenon. The ancient Greeks and Romans invented an entire panoply of gods and goddesses to blame for otherwise inexplicable events. Mars took the heat for war, Venus was behind passion's excesses and love gone wrong, Discordia sowed anger and conflict, Vulcan stoked up fires and volcanos, Neptune stirred angry seas and sent ships to the briny deep. Later, evil spirits, sorcerers, witches and various ethnic groups were charged with responsibility for human misery. More recently, Flip Wilson had a simpler, all-purpose explanation for his own offenses: the devil made me do it.

Finding someone to blame for misfortune provides a flood of relief. We can stop worrying and wondering. Anxiety and uncertainty, both distressing emotions, dissipate. Sometimes they're supplanted by anger, but anger's perceived as an invigorating emotion. Anger demands action and today many of us would rather act than think.

How does blame-seeking play out in 2022? America and the world find themselves confronted with disturbing trials and tribulations, circumstances unprecedented in number, gravity and confluence. This has generated a tsunami of blame-seeking. Worse, our problems have been exploited by unscrupulous politicians eager to harness our discontent to their own agendas by pointing the finger of blame at political opponents. In this context blame-seeking is better known as scapegoating.

Nobody wants to get sick or live in fear they or a loved one might sicken or die in the pandemic, so Covid becomes the Chinese Virus. China's to blame. We tire of being told to get vaccinated and boosted, we're unhappy wearing masks and staying home, so we ironically blame Dr. Fauci, Big Pharma or just government in general.

Some of us didn't like the result of the 2020 election so it must've been rigged. The election had to have been stolen by the same groups responsible for our changing demographics, evolving economy, lost jobs, gender issues, an opioid epidemic and rampant political correctness. It's those darn liberals, progressives, the deep state or all of them acting in concert. Plus, now they're the ones ramping up inflation. Blame it all on one big conspiracy. That's handy. You don't have to do the work of thinking through more complex issues. You don't have to face the painful realization that sometimes no-one's to blame, like the old bumper sticker advised, sometimes Sh** Happens.

Blame-seeking doesn't solve problems, doesn't find real answers. We're just having childlike tantrums, stamping our feet and demanding to get our way. As in the 1976 movie "Network" we want to scream "We're as mad as hell and we're not gonna take it anymore!" We're understandably angry but the problem is anger can balloon into rage and rage coupled with misdirected blame-seeking can result in irrational behavior, such as attacking the Capital and threatening your own elected representatives.

Then there's the invasion of Ukraine. It's a rare American who doesn't side with the Ukrainians standing up against a far superior Russian military. We all feel a need to somehow help these brave people. Most of us feel our country isn't doing enough but at the same time we don't want to send our kids in harm's way or risk setting off World War III by going head-to-head with Russia. We wish there were some solution to this dilemma and because none presents itself, blame-seeking kicks in. Whose fault is this? Is America weak? Is that the problem? If so, who's to blame? Maybe the President ought to, well, do something. Something more than he has. We have no idea what he should or could do, but we don't like having a feeling of helplessness free-floating around us. It has to settle somewhere. It has to be directed against someone. And so for many Americans the search for someone to blame, perversely enough begins and ends not with Vladimir Putin, but with Joe Biden.

Nobody said blame-seeking was logical.

Banned in Texas!

Our state is Number One in the race to ban books, according to Texas Monthly. It's not something we should view with pride. No trophies or ribbons are awarded the winner, nor is there a cash prize. Instead, we join the sordid ranks of governments, religions and others who've attempted over the years to dictate what others can and cannot read, see or hear. Their aim is to impose their values in place of a person's ability and responsibility to formulate their own opinions, judgments and decisions.

Although most of us would agree that certain sex-related topics should be off-limits to the very young, Texas lawmakers have gone way beyond that. PEN America says that between July, 2021 and late 2022, books were banned 1,229 times in Texas – far more than runner-up Florida. Maybe that's because some Texas legislators harbor odd notions of what subjects ought to be pulled from school library shelves. For example, according to the Dallas Observer, Matt Krause, formerly the 93rd District Texas House Representative, listed 850 novels he felt threatened young minds, including such salacious titles as Nancy Garden's *The Year They Burned the Books,* John Irving's *The Cider House Rules*, Louise Spilsbury's *Avoiding Bullies,* and Jacqueline Longe's *The Gale Encyclopedia of Medicine.*

This June, Governor Abbott signed into law HB900, the deceptively titled "Reader Act," imposing onerous requirements on vendors from whom public schools purchase books; an independent book store, for example. Under this law, The Mom & Pop Bookstore must read every book a school ever bought from them or might buy from them and assign a rating based on whether they believe it to be sexually explicit or sexually "relevant," whatever that might mean. Apparently, mom and pop are expected to find time to read cover-to-cover everything from *The Cat in the Hat* to *A Tale of Two Cities,* then report on where they feel it ranks on the Richter Scale of Sexuality. Quite a task. Then too, what if mom and pop find a book sexless, but Barnes and Noble proclaims it X-rated?

Sex, though, isn't the only thing worrying our legislators. They also enacted SB3 to shield students from the discomfort of any class discussion of a "widely debated and currently controversial issue of public policy or social affairs." A teacher who dares bring up such an issue is required to do so "objectively and free from bias." Sounds reasonable on the surface, but is it? Teachers in one North Texas school district were informed that any discussion of the Holocaust had to provide an "opposing" perspective. One wonders what that might look like. A treatise on the humanitarian intent of "Arbeit Macht Frei?"

SB3 also mandates that each ISD send a teacher and an administrator to a civics training program on how race and racism should be taught in schools. Maybe Texas could adopt the Florida model, which explains how slaves acquired valuable skills. Sure; skills like illiteracy, cotton-picking, submitting to rape, being whipped and swinging by the neck from a tree.

Sadly, the self-appointed censors in our State House are merely the latest link in a long and dismal chain of efforts at thought control through banning books or its kissing cousin, burning them. Way back in 212 BC the Chinese Emperor ordered all the books in his kingdom burned. Hebrew books were burned across the Italian states in 1533 as part of the Inquisition. Around the same time, Cardinal Wolsey forbade importing Martin Luther's books to England, while the Pope favored a bonfire instead. On May 10, 1933, a few years before they lit the ovens at Auschwitz-Birkenau, the Nazi's tossed thousands of books into bonfires in university towns all across Germany. The U.S. Library Journal responded, proudly adopting the motto, "In America we do not burn books, we build libraries." In Texas, though, when the state took over Houston ISD this year, libraries were converted to detention centers.

Historically, America has carried book banning to ridiculous extremes. Well into the 1950's, Boston led the effort, going so far as to ban an 1896 $5 bill that pictured partially nude allegorical figures. Spreading beyond Boston, the Comstock Act banned all "obscene materials" from the US mail, including any mention of birth control. "Comstockery" soon became synonymous with anti-intellectual puritanical priggishness.

In the final analysis, most book bans ultimately prove futile or even counter-productive. For years, a "Banned in Boston!" sticker on a book cover reliably supercharged sales. Now that we're leading the thought suppression sweepstakes, how long until we see books with DayGlo "Banned in Texas!" stickers?

𝔗he 𝔥olocaust

Each year one day recalls a time not long ago when men methodically exterminated entire populations not for anything they did, but simply for who they were. In Israel it is Yom HaShoah. Midmorning, a siren stops traffic. Drivers stand silently beside their vehicles. Nationwide, work and play abruptly halt. Heads are bowed, prayers recited.

In America, Holocaust Remembrance Day is less disruptive. Grisly death camp TV images and vows of "Never Again" attract a moment's notice on January 27, but unless we understand how the slaughter came about, we cannot prevent history from repeating itself.

Because it does, in Russian pogroms and gulags, in the Chinese Great Leap Forward, in Kosovo, in Cambodian killing fields, in Rwanda, in Somalia, and elsewhere. It is being repeated today in Syria. We may yet see it again in America, for our soil is not inhospitable to the poison seed of barbarism. It's flourished here in centuries of slavery, in Jim Crow lynchings, in the Trail of Tears, in the violent union-busting of the 1920's and other domestic atrocities. Perhaps these don't merit the term genocide, but what about next time? How might Holocaust 2026 come to pass?

History suggests the conflagration will build slowly. Most won't see it coming. In 1930's Germany the first steps were small, each curtailment of liberty, each restriction of freedom, each violation of the unwritten code of human decency portrayed as a necessary response to some fabricated threat. Finally, the Enabling Law granted Hitler power to rule by decree. An elected leader became the Fuhrer, a democracy a dictatorship.

Remarkably, Hitler's dreams of conquest solved Germany's chronic joblessness and economic malaise. Idle factories roared back to life building tanks, planes, ships and armament. The economy boomed and unemployment sunk to historic lows. To distract the population from the freedoms they were sacrificing to purchase prosperity, Hitler's cohort spread fear, concocting a panoply of "enemies of the people." Jews and Roma were labeled rapists and murderers. Homosexuals were stigmatized as degenerates unfit for Christian society. The disabled, the mentally ill and those unable to work were portrayed as a drain on the economy. The Nazis argued it might be best if these sub-humans were put away someplace. By the time the trains to Auschwitz began loading, few noticed or cared. The Holocaust's thousands of enablers were ordinary Germans leading workaday lives like ordinary Americans. That they were gears and cogs in a vast satanic machinery cranking out torture and death likely never crossed their minds. This casual thoughtlessness is what Hannah Arendt called the banality of evil.

Today we assume Americans would recognize the erosion of norms of civility which led to the Holocaust, but Sinclair Lewis's 1935 novel It Can't Happen Here, warned that such conceits are based more on hope than reality. Complacency corrodes the foundations of our republic and the decay is already underway. Hate groups have multiplied and many Americans feel alienated, unhappy with leaders who ignore their concerns. Simmering anger and frustration boiled over in 2016. No doubt many exited the voting booth thinking, "I showed 'em!"

It's a sentiment easily exploited, for those who manipulate the disaffected have technological tools today the Nazi's couldn't have imagined. The internet, social media and Big Data make it possible to inundate the public with propaganda disguised as news until the very notion of objective truth fades, animosity to opposing views mushrooms and critical thinking is drowned out by the persistent ranting of the peddlers of outrage and divisiveness.

In a coarser society, behavior once anathema has become commonplace, with verbal attacks an acceptable response to the bugaboo of political correctness. But verbal pummeling can escalate to physical violence and we're on the way to another Kristallnacht. It isn't difficult to imagine frightening scenarios for our future, as partisans bray for political opponents to be locked up. Once it's open season on dissent, how long until acrid smoke fills the air around Work Camps?

Alarmist? Perhaps, but Holocaust Remembrance Day <u>should</u> sound an alarm. Merely memorializing the Holocaust dead offers no prophylaxis against the metastatic disease that felled them. This cancer will not be cured with sympathy. Better to feel dread and fear; dread of the next outbreak and fear of the small but critical role each of us might play in spreading the contagion. If there is any hope of a vaccine against the virus of hatred and violence which humanity is now adept at incubating in pandemic proportions, it will be if the Holocaust reminds us that lulling conscience and critical thinking into a state of slumber is the first step to autocracy. We are all vulnerable to the sleep of reason, and it is there that monsters dwell.

Tom Kiske

𝓐 𝓟leasant 𝓦ay to 𝓓ie

"Gathering bones
on Hiroshima's burnt earth –
under the blazing sun."
Matsuo Atsuyuki, survivor

When the world's first nuclear explosion turned New Mexico's desert sand to glass July 16, 1945, witnesses were stunned by the devastation it wrought. Some openly wept. Lead scientist Robert Oppenheimer murmured a passage from the Bhagavd-Gita: "Now I am become death, the destroyer of worlds."

At 8:15 a.m. August 6, 1945 an atomic bomb was dropped on Hiroshima, Japan. Three days later a second one fell on Nagasaki. To the people of those cities Oppenheimer's words proved appallingly prophetic. The weapons were huge. The Nagasaki bomb, dubbed "Fat Man" exploded with the force of 21,000 tons of TNT. The fireball was hotter than the center of the sun; its blast waves carried twice the power of a Category 5 hurricane.

Thousands died immediately or within days. Death toll estimates vary, but could approach 200,000. More suffered horrible injuries. In her book, <u>Nagasaki</u>, Susan Southard describes the injuries to one child: "The entire left side of one little girl was badly burned, a bone stuck out of her right arm at the elbow, hundreds of glass splinters had penetrated most of her body, and blood was streaming down her neck." This was not atypical.

Beyond the blast, radiation sickness takes its own toll. First your hair falls out. Then it gets much worse. Your gums bleed, you have bloody diarrhea and vomit blood. Sometimes you bleed from your eyes. Lungs, kidneys and brains often hemorrhage. Ruptures occur in vital organs. Some blood cell counts drop to 50% of normal, others as low as 10%. Ulcerations develop in the larynx, bowels and elsewhere. Your skin can peel off. Your DNA is altered. You're in intense pain and then you die.

Testifying before the US Senate, the head of the Manhattan Project, General Leslie Groves, described radiation poisoning as "a very pleasant way to die." The facts were otherwise and he knew it.

The ethical and moral question remains: were we right to subject a largely civilian population to this horror?

Pearl Harbor, the Rape of Nanking, the Bataan Death March and other Japanese atrocities provoke a knee-jerk response. "Damn right we were. They brought this on themselves." Like many moral issues, though, the question bears deeper consideration. As John W. Philip, commanding the USS Texas, admonished his crew after sinking an enemy cruiser during the Spanish American War, "Don't cheer, boys. The poor devils are dying."

Not everyone involved with the war effort wanted to use the bomb. Some called for a demonstration explosion over an unpopulated area instead. Surely, they argued, this will convince the Japanese to surrender. Would that have worked and saved thousands of lives? Maybe, maybe not.

By late July, 1945 most of the Japanese high command knew the war was lost. With Emperor Hirohito's concurrence they had approached the Soviet Union to broker a surrender to the Allies. At the same time, though, they instructed their people to fight to the last man. Civilians were to arm themselves with bamboo spears to combat an invading army.

On July 26 the Allies issued the Potsdam Declaration, demanding unconditional surrender, warning the alternative would be Japan's "prompt and utter destruction." The Japanese didn't reply. Was that arrogance or did they just want time to craft a response? It was time they didn't have. President Truman had already issued the order to use the bombs, in part to strengthen our post-war negotiating stance with the USSR.

A different rationale was presented to the American public. We were told the alternative to the bomb meant invading the Japanese homeland, costing the lives of a million or more US soldiers, sailors and Marines.

My father was at that moment a Marine in the Philippines. No doubt he would have taken part in the invasion. Would he have made it home? Four of my uncles were also serving in the Pacific theater. Other relatives were aboard ships steaming to Japan. Years later my uncle Fred cut the Gordian Knot this way, "Harry Truman saved my life."

Still, we'll be well served if Christopher Nolan's <u>Oppenheimer</u> rekindles debate about the morality of what was done. Today, though, we face a more immediate nuclear question as Vladimir Putin threatens the use of so-called tactical nukes against Ukraine. In a war of his own making, however, ethical issues as well as legal ones are much clearer, and images of the aftermath of a nuclear strike would spread virally, searing the conscience of a world aghast. It's something the Russian leader, already facing arrest for war crimes, should weigh carefully. Surely there are already enough human bones to be gathered.

𝓦hy 𝓐re 𝓦e 𝓐ll 𝓢o 𝓐ngry?

Lately many op-eds ask why we're all so angry. That's not the question we should be asking ourselves though. A far better one for each of us is why am I so angry?

I was angered last week as I left the Larry Ringer library parking lot. For me a library is a sanctuary, a place I find calming. Since childhood I've loved wandering the shelves, pulling out a book here and there and skimming a few pages to decide if it's worth exploring further at home. What then could so quickly and utterly destroy my biblio-tranquility?

A big raised bed pickup truck roared by on Harvey Mitchell. It was the kind of truck you might've seen flying two Confederate battle flags. This one, though, sported just one flag; a large black one emblazoned with the sentiment, "F— Biden!" The f word was spelled out of course, and it wasn't "fudge." It's a word that has never and will never appear in *The Eagle* or any responsible publication out of respect for decency. Yet this guy felt justified waving it in the face of everyone he passed on public roads, including children. Imagine a little preschooler innocently asking, "Mommy, what's that flag say?"

I felt a visceral anger and outrage and as I drove homeward, I wondered exactly what it was it that got my Irish up. The affront to civility, of course, but more than that. What kind of person takes pride in flouting even a minimal standard of conduct? Even as an answer formed in my mind, I realize that as humans we have a tendency to categorize others, to assume that someone who does something we associate with a certain group automatically shares all the characteristics of that group. Do all Democrats favor open borders and expansive entitlements; all Republicans endorse book banning and voter suppression? Of course not. By the same token why do I assume anyone who'd drive around flying an obscene black flag is the kind of guy who would've donned a white sheet and hung strange fruit from Southern trees or helped stoke the ovens at Auschwitz?

In truth I know nothing about that pickup driver. Maybe he's a fine fellow who regularly attends church, loves his kids and donates generously to charity. He just doesn't like the President of the United States. <u>Really</u> doesn't like him and wants everyone to know it. Doesn't give a flip whether others share his opinion or not, because, well, free speech and all that. Musk has Twitter, this guy has a pickup and a flag. F word aside, it's his right as an American, so maybe I ought to be happy with his confirmation of that right no matter how flagrant and tawdry.

Intellectually, perhaps, and on that level, I simply want to ask him what Biden had done to incite his hatred. In my gut though, I feel more like flipping him off. Extreme gestures evoke extreme reactions. A lot of violence begins that way.

I'm still stewing when I get home to find my neighbor has put a sign in his yard for a certain state office candidate. It's a candidate I don't like. I think about getting a yard sign for his opponent. I consider the pros and cons of doing this, eventually deciding it's not a great idea. It would be an escalation and a provocation. My neighbor's sign doesn't arouse anywhere near the ire of the black flag.

Why is that? Maybe because unlike pickup guy, I do know my neighbors. I know them to be good, decent folks who simply have different political beliefs than mine. I value our friendship and enjoy our occasional chats. We call on each other for small favors from time to time. I keep an eye on their house when they're away and they do the same for me.

In 2022 America we too often see our political opponents as enemies. They're not. They're fellow citizens whose views differ from ours. In an ideal world we'd be able to engage with them in reasoned, dispassionate debate and perhaps find some common ground. It could happen. It's happened many times before in American history or we would never have become the nation we are, for all our flaws still a force for good in a world too often drawn to the dark side.

But even when we cannot agree and compromise seems elusive, surely, we can step back, shake hands with our opponents, treat them with respect and remain on friendly terms. Can't we? Please. Lest the atavistic simian side of our nature undo us all.

Tom Kiske

Watch Their Language

As a child your mom may have occasionally cautioned you to watch your language. A wise mother might've added watch their's too. Her first warning was probably about profanity. The second, though, was of far greater consequence: don't let other people's words fool you. Her counsel is especially relevant in 2022 as language is increasingly used to manipulate beliefs and behavior. Our schools could do more to arm future consumers and voters against verbal chicanery.

For many years European education followed classical tradition, focused on three elements: grammar, logic and rhetoric. These guides and the one thing common to all - language - equipped one to navigate through life, employing reason to acquire and acquire ideas and opinions while avoiding persuasive pitfalls and snares set for the unwary.

How can language be used to mislead? Examples go back thousands of years. In Genesis 3:14 the serpent tells Eve if she eats the fruit of a certain tree she'll be like God. Consequences ensue. Around 800 BCE Homer writes that Odysseus blinds the cyclops, then tells Polyphemus his name is Nobody. When Polyphemus yells ANobody has injured me@ his fellow one-eyed giants don't rush to his aid. Fortunate for the Greeks, not so much for Polyphemus.

Nowadays, those who wish to influence behavior use subtler tactics. Advertisers, for example, have honed the art of persuasive language to a science. A cheery TV spokesperson announces, AThe more you spend, the more you save!@ But isn't spending the opposite of saving? The truth is the more you spend, the more you spend. Similarly, a dietary supplement claims it supports cellular health. Perhaps so, but so does a glass of water or a burger.

Many products are advertised as natural, implying they're safe. A sip of natural cyanide or strychnine would convince you otherwise. The active ingredient in benign-sounding Botox is botulinum toxin, the world's deadliest natural poison, ok only if administered sparingly by a qualified physician. A mere milligram would be fatal if swallowed.

In recent years, politicians and activists of all stripes have adopted many of the linguistic tactics of unscrupulous advertisers. On the Republican side, in the 80's Newt Gingrich convinced his party that the key to victory was to tar their enemies with catchy nicknames and carefully crafted attack lines. Gingrich also insisted Republicans use the epithet Democrat Party in lieu of Democratic which he felt sounded too close to democracy. That was just the start, though. Through GOPAC, he circulated a memo entitled ALanguage: A Key Mechanism of Control@ which provided an extensive list of pejorative terms for use in describing Democrats: radical, corrupt, self-serving, etc. The political consultant Frank Luntz added a few more: say death tax instead of estate tax, energy exploration, not oil drilling, he suggested. Today this idea has mushroomed to include absurdities like Kellyanne Conway's alternative facts.

While the Democratic Party didn't publish a preferred vocabulary of dysphemisms to use against opponents, neither did they abjure labels like Tricky Dick for Richard Nixon or characterizing the GOP as a restricted country club for wealthy WASPs. Moreover, leftist academics and activists twisted language to their own ends with extremes of political correctness.

Increasingly, the two major parties employ different, value-laden terms to talk about fundamental concepts. Is our economic system capitalism or free enterprise? Is it healthcare reform or socialized medicine? Are progressive tax rates a way to ensure all pay their fair share or a confiscatory program of wealth distribution? The trouble is language is our primary means of communication. Intentionally corrupting it means pressing societal issues cannot be rationally and dispassionately discussed, alternative solutions openly debated and, with a bit of mutual goodwill, problems solved.

Instead, with the election season gearing up here in the Lone Star, commercials feature candidates trying to outdo each other in

227

fighting for Texas values. Setting aside that most of us might prefer reasoning and compromise to all that fighting, exactly what are those Texas values? Well, football, of course, but beyond that many Texans would be surprised to learn their values aren't universally shared. We're a far more diverse state than years ago. Some of us are pro-life, some pro-choice; some favor open carry, others prefer control of fire arms; some think open elections invite fraud, others think restricting suffrage is restricting democracy.

There may be a few commonly held values - honesty, integrity, justice and tolerance come to mind - but you don't often see those in campaign ads. Why not? Them ain't fightin' words.

In Wonderland, Alice tells Humpty Dumpty, "The question is whether you can make words mean different things." She recognizes he's using words deceptively. In word wonderland 2022 we should be no less discerning. Watch their language.

Is the Light Going Out?

In school we were taught there was a time in the latter half of the 17th Century when Europe and the West began to emerge from ignorance and superstition and learned the power of reason and rationality. It was known as The Enlightenment and America, perhaps more than any other country, became the beneficiary of that great movement. The self-evident truths identified in the Declaration of Independence and the radical notion that government power should come not from a divinely designated monarch but from the consent of the governed confirm that the founders of our experiment in democracy were surely and devotedly children of The Enlightenment.

Our nation grew and prospered not only because of the freedoms enshrined in our founding documents but also from The Enlightenment's spirit of unfettered inquiry into the nature of the world in which we live. Science emerged and the scientific method quickly proved a better tool for problem solving than reliance on ancient texts and received "wisdom." New discoveries and inventions improved living conditions. Wealth and the benefits wealth affords were no longer the exclusive privilege of kings and nobles but were better distributed among common folks. The idea of progress took hold and ordinary people began to expect that their lives would continue to improve over time.

To be sure, science also produced new and terrible weapons. Warfare went global in the 20th Century and for the first time we became capable of eradicating our species and poisoning our planet. Some say such poisoning is already underway, not through weapons of mass destruction, but as an unforeseen side effect of an avaricious drive for abundance - a pursuit that left many behind.

Still, few would argue for a return to pre-scientific thought. At least not outwardly; not in such straightforward terms. There are those, however, who find certain scientific conclusions inconvenient, disruptive. Those who deny the amply demonstrated truth of climate change and the potentially disastrous consequences of a significantly warmer Earth are a case in point. Worse, the widespread resistance to science-based measures to contain the Covid-19 pandemic hinted that the light of The Enlightenment might be dimming. Sadly, many of us remain creatures more ruled by poorly articulated passions than reason. We want our lives to continue as we have known them, accumulating without pause the luxuries of an energy-dependent prosperity. We want football, open shops, restaurants and bars. We don't want to wear masks. We want it all back the way it was and we want it now!

Thus some blindly dismiss the very science that made our lifestyle possible, turning instead to populist political leaders who assure us pandemics aren't so bad, will magically disappear next month and are probably the work of a heinous conspiracy of child sex traffickers. This may sound far-fetched, but recent Pew polls found a quarter of Americans say there's some truth to the idea that the Covid-19 pandemic was intentionally planned. Less than half of Americans and only 27% of Republicans expressed a great deal of trust in scientists.

Science is fine as long as it gives us what we want. When it conflicts with our desires we cast science aside and revert to the old ways. We deny what we don't like, ignore what is uncomfortable to confront and then conjure fanciful stories to rationalize our irrationality. We close our eyes to what is and instead inhabit an imaginary world free of troubling facts, where everything would be wonderful if only everyone were exactly like us.

How will this disturbing trend play out in our hyper-partisan environment? Do we still believe in the self-evident truths articulated in 1776 and reflected in Article 1 of the U.N.'s Universal Declaration of Human Rights, which declares, "All human beings are born free and equal in dignity and rights. They are endowed with reason and conscience and should act towards one another in a spirit of brotherhood."

Are we still guided by The Enlightenment or is its thin filament failing? Is the light flickering, dimming, threatening to go dark? Will we allow Yeats' "rough beast" of ignorance, superstition and prejudice, "its hour come 'round at last" to slouch toward America?" We, of course, means you and me, and November 3 may foretell if sunrise or sunset lies ahead.

Tom Kiske

𝕭ias

Letters accusing *The Eagle* of bias are not uncommon on the Opinions page. Some detect a liberal bias; others claim the newspaper leans right. Regardless of the perceived direction of tilt, what is meant is that the publication deliberately and consciously presents articles favoring one political persuasion over another. It's unlikely many outraged letter writers realize that what they see as *The Eagle*'s conscious bias may well instead reflect one or more of their own unconscious biases.

Like dark matter in the physical universe, in the mental and intellectual universe, the realm of unconscious or implicit bias far exceeds that of the kind more easily, if often mistakenly, exposed. It influences our perceptions, our thinking and our judgement. We're all vulnerable to it and if you believe you're not, chances are you're more susceptible than most. We can't escape it, but by becoming aware of it we can mitigate its influence and the possibility that manipulative agents might weaponize our hidden biases, logical flaws and undeveloped critical thinking skills for their own purposes.

Over the years, psychologists have identified scores of what might be termed dark biases, flawed patterns of thinking that lurk beneath the level of consciousness. Entire books have been written on the subject, including Rolf Dobelli's popular The Art of Thinking Clearly. A few of the more common ones follow.

Perhaps the single most prevalent unconscious bias is the confirmation bias. It works like this: if, for whatever reason, you believe *The Eagle* to be a tool of the liberal elite, perhaps even part of the scurrilous Amainstream media, you will find ample instances to confirm that belief while ignoring contrary evidence. Similarly, if you believe blacks are thugs or immigrants are rapists and murderers, your mind will selectively cull news reports to reinforce that belief despite facts and statistics which prove otherwise.

The Recency Bias inclines us to give more weight to what happened today than last month. A conservative article in today's Eagle far outweighs a liberal one we barely remember from a week ago and is therefore stronger evidence our local newspaper is a right-wing propaganda organ.

What's known as the Affect Heuristic describes the human tendency for a strong positive or negative emotional reaction to overrule reason. The best example of this is a study showing that given a choice between a medical treatment that will save 95 out of a hundred patients versus one that will allow 5 out of a hundred to die, people see the latter as a far worse option. The Affect Heuristic also explains why personal anecdotes seem to carry more impact than dry statistics. Someone telling you, "I drank peanut oil daily and never caught Covid-19" exerts a more visceral response than "A dozen studies found peanut oil ineffective." It also explains why one political campaign features Mary, whose daughter was assaulted by an undocumented immigrant while another campaign highlights Jose, whose lack of documentation didn't hold him back from becoming a neurosurgeon.

The Law of Small Numbers is a statistical quirk often exploited by opinion writers to persuade readers that facts support their view of things. For example, you might read that small schools provide a better education because statistically they produce a higher percentage of high-achieving students. Although that's true it's misleading because small schools also produce a high percentage of low-achieving students. How can this be? Easy. 50 high or low achieving students represent 5% of a school with five hundred kids, but only 1% of a school with 2500 kids. Most students fall in the middle, regardless of school size. It's just that in small schools, outliers stand out more.

Similar to the Affect Heuristic, Framing Effects also distort our judgement because of how facts are presented. Shoppers given a choice between a product that's 5% fat or one that's 95% fat-free overwhelmingly choose the latter. It just sounds better even though we know the products are identical.

These implicit biases don't mean people are stupid. We live in an age of information overload. Most of us are busy earning a living and caring for our families. With a limited amount of time to carefully evaluate the news, opinions and advertising that assault us every waking hour, our minds take shortcuts. In a nutshell, that's what implicit biases are: mental shortcuts. Unfortunately, they aren't always pathways to understanding and truth. Too often they lead to a distorted worldview. This then becomes the lens through which virtually everything is seen. We judge right and wrong, friend and enemy based on consistency with our ill-conceived worldview.

There's a certain warm comfort that comes from no longer having to think through complex issues and risk the worry that thoughtful analysis might shatter our fundamental assumptions and long-held opinions. But is it better to live within a pleasant illusion or to confront what Al Gore famously referred to as an inconvenient truth?

Is *The Eagle* biased? I think not but cannot claim absolute certainty. What I do know for sure is that you and I are biased, whether consciously or not.

Our Long, Hot Summer

Hot enough for you?

By any measure, the Brazos Valley's long, hot summer has been one for the record books: the hottest highs, the warmest morning lows, the most severe drought conditions. Seventy-four days over 100 degrees; July, August, lingering through the end of September. Fifteen days over 105 degrees. An all-time high temperature of 112 degrees hit twice, August 20 and 27.

What will we suffer through next summer and the summer after that? 118? 125? Maybe we're closer to that than we think. Our official readings are taken at Easterwood airport, but in the downtown areas of Bryan and College Station, the "heat island" effect means temps 6 degrees hotter than in suburban or rural areas. Our official high of 112 might be more like 118 where development is more dense.

Something unusual seems to be going on, doesn't it? Something worrisome. Why is this happening? What does it mean?

Remember local TV meteorologists mentioning the high pressure "heat dome" that lingered over Texas almost all summer? That's the culprit behind both summer's sizzling temperatures and the drought. But why did it get stuck right here over our sweaty heads?

When you look under the hood, so to speak, you realize that our local weather is driven by several large, complex and interconnected systems, beginning with the jet stream high in the atmosphere, moving generally west to east across the US. It doesn't run in a straight line, though. It meanders in troughs and ridges pushing areas of high and low pressure, and the whole thing depends on the difference in temperature between the poles and the tropics.

The problem is, all those intricate interactions are being disrupted by the overall warming of our planet. Because the north pole is warming four times faster than other areas, that crucial north-south temperature gradient is weakened, so the jet stream wobbles around more than normal. This makes it vulnerable to a phenomenon known as atmospheric blocking, which can lock weather patterns in place for months. Like our infamous heat dome

But to some folks, summer 2023 is not big deal. "Summertime's always hot in Texas," they say. True, but not like this. The upward trend is ominous, but politicians fiddle while America burns

Heat can and does kill. In the summer of 2021, downtown Portland, Oregon jumped from 76 degrees to 114, resulting in a thousand deaths officially and likely more. In 2003, Paris temperatures were over 95 degrees for 9 days, spiking to 104 and causing 15,000 deaths. Worldwide in 2019, extreme heat caused 489,000 deaths, according to The Lancet.

Still, many will dismiss these heat-related casualties, thinking, I'll just crank up the a/c. A few problems with that notion. First, the higher the temperature, the less efficient your a/c. Dr. Andrew Dressler, a climate scientist at Texas A&M, has said that when the outside temperature goes from 95 to 98, air conditioners use 30% more power to maintain an inside temperature of 75 degrees. Your electric bill will mirror the increase. And how much more when the outside temp hits 112? Plus, your condenser is actually spewing hot air into the atmosphere, potentially making the situation worse.

Secondly, our cool comfort is completely reliant on technology and an infrastructure that may not be up to the task. Remember how often Ercot issued advisories asking us to reduce usage? We avoided rolling blackouts this summer, but will our luck hold when summer temperatures go to 120? Heat is the enemy of electric transmission, including the lines that bring power to our homes. If it gets hot enough, transformers will begin to blow. No power, no a/c. And if the grid fails as it did in the winter of 2021, how many will die here in the Brazos Valley and across Texas?

To its credit, in 2022 the city of College Station adopted and began implementing a five-year program to mitigate the heat island effect, primarily by planting hundreds, if not thousands of trees. Unfortunately, the planting had to be paused due to the exceptional drought. College Station is also examining alternative water supplies, realizing our aquifers are under stress. These are good first steps Bryan should also consider.

Are they enough? Time will tell. We're still close to 100 degrees in October, but cooler days are coming and maybe we'll forget about our sizzling summer. But maybe if we sweat through markedly higher temps next year or the year after, maybe if we lose power or don't have enough water to drink, maybe then it will finally be hot enough for us. Hot enough for all of us to not only feel the heat, but to see the light.

Veterans Day

My father had already received his draft notice and passed his physical when I was born in August of '43. A week later my mom and dad and their newborn son rode the bus to Union Station where he boarded the train that would take him to San Diego. When my mother waved goodbye, she didn't know when – or if - she would see him again. Already 34 years old, he was headed to boot camp with boys half his age. A few weeks later he'd be among the 62 members of the 716th Platoon, U. S. Marine Corps, shipping out to battle America's World War II enemies in the Pacific. They'd be in it for the duration; for however long the war went on.

These were hard times both for those who went off to war and for those left behind. Men in the military signed over part of their meager pay to take care of their families. Often it was most of their paycheck. For new guys, before their wives or mothers saw a cent of what was called an Allotment, the paperwork had to find its way through a vast bureaucracy. My mom waited almost two months, juggling bills for rent, utilities and groceries for herself and baby. At the point of desperation, she asked the Red Cross for help. A couple of weeks later they sent her two tickets for a midnight movie at the Fox theater.

Where do you turn when you're a new mother with no money? My father's older sister lived across the courtyard. Did my mom approach that stern woman for a loan? I don't know. I do know my aunt wrote my dad overseas complaining his wife wasn't keeping her windows clean. Helpful?

Fortunately, just across the street was a small grocery store run by Mr. Ketter, a kind man. Many folks in the neighborhood were like us, living hand to mouth. At Ketter's we could run a tab, get the food to sustain us with no more than a promise to pay when we were able. It kept many from starvation, and if you noticed a little green at the end of the bologna Ketter was slicing for you he'd just chop off that part with a smile. No problem.

His little grocery store was also a vital communication link. It's difficult today to imagine, but a telephone was a luxury back then few could afford. Ketter took calls for the entire neighborhood. If an important call came in for someone living close by, Ketter would stand outside his door and yell, "Mrs. Jones – phone call!" Mrs. Jones would come running. Ketter never made anyone feel they were imposing on him. He was happy to help. It was what people were supposed to do in hard times.

When my mom finally started getting her monthly allotment check, it was enough to cover our basic needs but because virtually the entire economy was devoted to the war effort, many common items were strictly rationed. The government issued ration coupons that permitted you to buy, for example, only so much milk or butter each month. You had to surrender the corresponding coupon to the grocery store before paying for your stick of butter.

Scarcity was widespread. It was part of the price the civilian population paid to support the troops. The price GI's paid month after month, year after year on battlefields far from home, was far higher. Like most, my father never spoke of what he went through.

What he did, though, was write to his son from somewhere in the South Pacific on October 13, 1944. His letter tells me he misses me and says "I never knew how much you were to me until now." He goes on, "Tell your mom to make sure you have a nice Christmas even though I cannot be there to help you celebrate it." He cautions me to eat my cereal and drink my milk so I can grow up husky and take care of my mother. He wants me to go to church so I'll ". . . be a God fearing fellow and not get into too much trouble". In conclusion he writes, "I want you to learn that all men are alike whether they are white or black Mohamedan (sic) or Christian. Do everything you can to make all men respect you." His letter is signed simply, "I Am Your Dad."

I would be a toddler by the time Sergeant Kiske saw his son again.

𝕬uthor 𝕭io

Tom Kiske came to Earth as an infant in 1943 as the planet was engulfed in war. His mission was to embed himself in the local population of the dominant species and, as he grew, observe human conditions, analyze them and periodically report back to Starfleet Command for evaluation and appropriate action. Initially, his reports were crisp, factual and objective, however as time passed, he became perhaps overly-imbedded, acquiring a great deal of sympathy for the human condition and even some admiration for certain members of the species, especially after the odd metamorphosis known as puberty.

At length, Kiske even married an Earth girl, which he attempted to characterize in his reports as "research," but which fooled no-one. Admiral Spock immediately recognized that the mission had been compromised and ordered the fleet to regroup, withdraw and reconsider whether or not the whole business was worth additional time and effort.

Meanwhile, Kiske continues to dutifully continue his reports. This book is his most recent.

www.ingramcontent.com/pod-product-compliance
Lightning Source LLC
Chambersburg PA
CBHW020359030726
47496CB00007B/2208